LEGAL PRACTICE HANDBOOK

EFFECTIVE
COMMUNICATION

LEGAL PRACTICE HANDBOOK

EFFECTIVE COMMUNICATION

Anthony G. King, MA, Solicitor

Director of Education
Clifford Chance

Series Editor: Anthony G. King

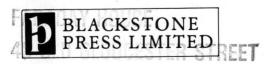

BLACKSTONE
PRESS LIMITED

First published in Great Britain 1992 by Blackstone Press Limited,
9-15 Aldine Street, London W12 8AW. Telephone 081-740 1173

© Anthony G. King, 1992

ISBN: 1 85431 165 4

British Library Cataloguing in Publication Data
A CIP catalogue record for this book is available from the British
Library

Typeset by Style Photosetting Ltd, Mayfield, East Sussex
Printed by BPCC Wheatons Ltd, Exeter

Contents

Contents

Preface

Effective Communication has been written with a view to helping any lawyer wanting to hone his or her presentation skills. I hope it will be useful to trainee solicitors new to the office environment; I also hope it will help more senior lawyers who have to make presentations at beauty parades or conferences.

Many of the ideas in the book stem from my personal lecturing experiences. I have, therefore, approached the book from the viewpoint of identifying what I would have liked to have known when I began making presentations. I trust I have covered everything, but responsibility for any omissions or errors is mine and mine alone.

I am grateful to my many colleagues, past and present, for all the help and guidance they have given to me.

I would like to give particular thanks to my wife for her support at all times. Finally, I would like to thank Alistair MacQueen, Heather Saward and everyone at Blackstone Press Limited for their ideas, support and, most important of all, their patience.

Tony King
London

Introduction

Were one of the national opinion pollsters to conduct a survey to identify the general public's perception of a lawyer's key skill, it is a reasonable assumption that most of those questioned would identify it as 'being skilful with words'. If that is the case, why is it that a common complaint about individual lawyers (including those received by the Solicitors' Complaints Bureau) is: 'It was obvious that he knew what he was talking about but I could not understand a word of it'?

The answer lies in the quote from the disgruntled client. The majority of lawyers will, quite correctly, devote considerable time and energy to ensure they achieve technical excellence in their field of speciality. However, when it comes to explaining some aspect of their speciality, they fail to use the techniques which would help them get their message across effectively.

The purpose of this book is to explain these techniques in a practical way for the benefit of lawyers, irrespective of the stage they have reached in their careers. Nevertheless, the book is principally aimed at young lawyers starting out on their careers whose experience of explaining complex legal issues to their professional colleagues and clients is relatively limited. It is also hoped that more experienced lawyers will be able to hone their existing skills using the techniques outlined in this book. The book is also designed to help any lawyer who is required to give formal presentations such as at a beauty parade or a training session.

When deciding on a title for this book, there was a lengthy debate between the author and the publishers on whether it should be called 'Effective Presentation' or the more general title 'Effective Communication'. The former title gives the immediate impression that this book is about *oral* communication (which is indeed its purpose). Unfortunately, the title carries with it the impression that it is aimed solely at the skills required for formal presentations at lectures. A lecture is perhaps the most obvious circumstance in which effective oral communication skills are required but it is not the only circumstance. Therefore, it was with a view to emphasising the wider relevance of this skill that the more general title of 'Effective Communication' was chosen.

In the succeeding chapters, the book will explain the techniques for ensuring that the speaker's ideas and messages are presented effectively. Chapter 1 will illustrate the wide range of circumstances in which these presentation techniques can be used.

Having defined in a very wide sense in chapter 1 what a 'presentation' is, chapter 2 examines the factors to take into account when going through the initial stages of preparing for any presentation. Chapter 3 examines the techniques for structuring any presentation as well as examining the necessity for and techniques of rehearsing a presentation.

Chapter 4 gives guidance on the actual delivery of the information. The chapter examines some devices for helping the audience understand the speaker's message as well as the physical aspects of presenting information such as the use of the voice, eye contact and methods for conquering nerves.

Chapter 5 examines the use of visual aids and gives guidance on making the most effective use of the wide variety of types of visual aid available to any speaker. Other technological aids to presentations (such as amplification) are examined together with guidance on the use of documentation to support any presentation.

For many speakers the most nerve-wracking aspect of giving a presentation is dealing with the questions which can arise after they have 'said their piece'. Chapter 6 examines the techniques for dealing with questions as well as looking at a number of logistical problems which can arise both before and during the presentation. The same chapter also examines the logistical aspects of giving presentations and gives guidance on points to check with regard to the venue for the presentation, the equipment supplied and points to be agreed with any co-presenters.

The ability to communicate effectively is truly transferable in that the techniques explained in this book can be applied whatever the circumstance in which the 'presentation' is to be made and whatever the subject-matter of the 'presentation'. The techniques can, therefore, be applied when giving information on a non-legal subject just as easily as they can be applied to a legal presentation. Having said that, this book has been written with lawyers in mind.

Although lawyers communicate both orally and in writing this book only addresses the issues of effective *oral* communication. Guidance on effective *written* communication skills is to be found in *Legal Writing and Legal Drafting* text in the Legal Practice Series. At the end of this book is a bibliography listing additional reading on presentation skills.

Chapter One

Why Are Effective Communication Skills Necessary and When Are They Used?

1.1 WHY IS IT NECESSARY TO BE A GOOD COMMUNICATOR?

To practise as a lawyer, whatever your area of expertise, you need to acquire a comprehensive command of the technicalities and practicalities of your chosen area of specialisation. Any lawyer who does not strive to achieve this cannot hope to be given the accolade of being regarded as a 'good lawyer' by his colleagues or clients. However, no matter how good your command of the technicalities and practicalities of your chosen area may be, your abilities will not be recognised if you cannot communicate your expertise.

In our increasingly competitive, recession-hit world, the importance of the ability to communicate effectively cannot be underestimated. In the race for promotion within firms and the race to gain and retain clients, technical expertise is often assumed. Therefore, the factor which determines whether an individual is promoted to partnership, or a firm wins business from a client, is often whether the individual or the firm can display the range of non-technical skills covered in the books in this series. While all the skills covered in the series are important, a crucial weapon in any lawyer's armoury is the ability to communicate effectively.

This idea that your personal and interpersonal skills are at least as important, if not more important, than your technical skills is not new. Lord Curzon, one of the greatest public speakers of his day, used to advise colleagues about to speak in public that there were three important factors to bear in mind when presenting to an audience. In order of importance, those factors are:

(a)   Who you are.

(b)   How you say it.

(c)   What you say.

At first sight, it may seem extraordinary that content is at the bottom of this particular list. However, everyone has experience of listening to knowledgeable speakers who present their talks in such a boring, incomprehensible or disorganised manner as to make the presentation worthless. Lord Curzon's precepts, particularly the importance of the way the information is delivered, continue to be used by our modern-day political leaders. The communications adviser to the former Prime Minister, Mrs Margaret Thatcher, used to advise her that presentation constitutes 90 per cent of the impact of any speech while content amounts to only 10 per cent. While these percentages may not have been scientifically tested, the old adage, 'It's not what you say, it's the way that you say it' continues to hold good.

The advice given by Mrs Thatcher's communications adviser clearly cannot be rigidly applied by a lawyer who is trying to get across technical information. The content aspect clearly must represent more than 10 per cent of the total impact of the presentation. However, the general principle, that at least equal weight must be given to the method of presentation as to the content of the presentation, is irrefutably true.

Your colleagues and clients will assume you know your law (unless you give them clear evidence to the contrary); it is the way you communicate your knowledge or display your expertise that they will remember. Therefore, if you appear to be knowledgeable, to be on top of your subject and to be in control of the situation, people will accept the image you are projecting. The image you project to your colleagues or clients will give them an impression of you. Your image will be inextricably bound up with the image you are projecting of your firm or the organisation for which you work, irrespective of your status. If you impress the client, by association the client will be impressed with your firm. From this will flow obvious benefits in terms of business opportunities for the firm as well as potential promotion opportunities for you.

1.2   WHAT IS A PRESENTATION?

Before examining the techniques which you can employ to be an 'effective communicator', you need to understand the circumstances in which those skills are needed.

In the minds of most people, the question 'What is a presentation?' will conjure up a picture of a 'formal' lecture delivered by an 'expert' to a relatively large audience. The detail of these mental pictures will vary; for some people a presentation conjures up memories of their school-days, for others the mental picture is of a university lecture or, in these days of the Law Society's Continuing Education Scheme, a speech organised by one of the commercial providers of legal education courses.

Whatever the detail of the picture, the image is usually of a tutor delivering information to the serried ranks of a largely passive audience. This approach (sometimes called the 'talking-head' approach) certainly falls within the definition of a 'presentation'. However, a lecture is merely one type of presentation and the 'talking-head' approach merely one type of approach which can be adopted. (It is perhaps the least effective way of ensuring the audience assimilates the information being delivered.)

To give a better idea of circumstances when effective communication skills can be used, it may be helpful to give the term 'presentation' a simple, but comprehensive, definition:

Any circumstance in which ideas and/or information are communicated orally by one person to one or more others.

Fuller illustrations of 'presentations' are given in 1.3 below but, following this definition, you will be making a 'presentation' whenever you communicate any information or ideas about yourself, your work or your firm to anyone else.

1.3 WHEN WILL YOU USE EFFECTIVE COMMUNICATION SKILLS?

The following paragraphs discuss some situations in which lawyers need effective communication skills, and highlight points of general relevance to presentations. The techniques described in this book can be used in all the situations outlined in this section.

1.3.1 Giving instructions to colleagues

Whatever your status within your firm or organisation, on a daily or even hourly basis you will be giving instructions to your colleagues or juniors. These can range from simple instructions or requests (such as to your secretary to return to a colleague a file you have borrowed) to complex instructions on delegated work or requests for assistance on a topic outside your area of technical expertise. Both situations count as presentations albeit that the effort involved in the former may be minimal as compared to the latter. In the case of the former it is a simple matter to identify the file and the colleague to whom you want it returned. However, you must take care to ensure you give your secretary all the information she requires. If you gave her the instruction on your dictating machine, is the instruction audible when she plays back the tape? (Far too many 'presentations' have lost all their impact by being inaudible to the audience.) Identifying the file clearly is not enough if you do not make it clear to your secretary precisely where in your office she can find the file. (Many speakers lose their audience by not appreciating the audience's pre-existing level of knowledge of the subject.) Identifying the colleague to whom the file should be returned by his or her first name when there are several people with that first name to whom the file could be returned can, at best, lead to time being wasted. (Many negligence actions brought against lawyers have arisen because the lawyer had in mind one course of action but, due to a misunderstanding or a lack of effective communication, a client followed another course.)

On the face of it, delegating a complex task to a junior lawyer or seeking assistance from one of your colleagues would seem to be an entirely different situation from the previous example. However, the issues involved in communicating effectively are virtually identical. What is the task you are trying to delegate or the matter on which you want assistance? (You must identify the objective of your 'presentation' in advance.) Not giving time to prepare to give your instructions or pass on your request will inevitably lead to time being wasted and, possibly, confusion arising. What information does your junior or colleague need to deal with your task? You must review the facts and sift them with a view to extracting only the relevant information. Having identified the relevant facts, will your junior or colleague know what it is you expect them to do and by when? (In too many presentations, the audience is left with an understanding of the information delivered but may not necessarily know what to do with that information.)

Instructions to colleagues are often given face to face and so you will have the benefit of being able to read the body language of your junior or colleague to see whether they understand. An understanding of the body language signals we all transmit is essential if you are to maximise the impact of face-to-face communication.

1.3.2   Giving advice to your clients

Many lawyers would regard giving advice to their clients, whether over the telephone or in a meeting, more as a discussion or as an interview than a presentation. It is true that this situation may require techniques in addition to those covered by the 'effective communication' heading, for example, the ability to interview effectively (covered by Helena Twist's book, *Effective Interviewing*, in this series). However, at some stage in the process you will have to give advice to the client. This stage is a presentation pure and simple. The client will need to be convinced that you understand his or her problem. You will, therefore, need to be able to explain your understanding of the factual basis of that problem clearly and concisely. Given that factual background, you will have to examine the possible solutions to the problem in a way which the client will understand. The client may be commercially sophisticated (for example, where you are advising a commercial property developer on structuring a new deal). In that case you must ensure you express yourself in a way which will reassure the client that you understand business at the client's level. Alternatively, you may be dealing with a battered wife who is seeking a divorce or an injunction. Such a client may have had no contact with a lawyer before and have no appreciation of the technicalities or practicalities of the law. You must adjust the level of technicality of your presentation to fit her level of understanding.

Having explained the options, you should give the client advice in the sense of giving your view of the best course to follow. The client is paying you for advice, not simply a review of the relevant law. The client will, therefore, expect to be given guidance on what he or she should do and not be left to choose from several different alternatives, perhaps none of which he or she fully understands. In any presentation, it is important to draw conclusions from the information you are presenting. Without a conclusion, whether it is advice to a client on future action to take in respect of a particular problem or a key message you are trying to get across in a training programme, your presentation will be incomplete.

A service which lawyers often supply to their clients is the preparation of documents. The meeting with the client may involve an explanation of a document the client has to sign. In this circumstance, you will have to identify the best approach for explaining the document to the client. Is it sufficient to simply let the client read the document? Should you merely explain the structure of the document or its key points? Many lawyers find it impossible, both in meetings and in lectures, to refrain from giving a complete picture of whatever it is they are trying to explain. Does the client really need to know the background to *Re Sinclair* when you are explaining a few words from the clause in a will dealing with a substitutional gift? Would it not be better simply to explain the effect?

Neither you nor your 'audience' will want the presentation to go on too long. Therefore you should always approach the presentation with a view to delivering the *key* information within the time available. Keeping to time is an essential element of communicating effectively.

1.3.3   Putting your client's case across to others

Stating your client's position in the opening stages of a negotiation, or your client's case in your opening speech in court, both amount to presentations. You will need to prepare properly for these presentations by understanding the key issues and presenting them in an appropriate order.

In these two circumstances other skills (namely, negotiation and advocacy) are needed. For a more detailed explanation of each of those skills, the reader is referred to Ann Halpern's *Effective Negotiation* and Avrom Sherr's *Advocacy* in this series.

1.3.4   Helping clients to make or save a deal

In some commercial transactions, the clients use their legal advisers to help them make or save deals. The client may work with the lawyer to structure a deal in a particular way and then, in conjunction with the lawyer, 'sell' the deal to other parties. This can apply, for example, to joint ventures or syndications of loans by banks. These 'selling' presentations will usually be a joint effort between the client and the lawyer. The client will explain the commercial aspects of the deal and the lawyer will explain the legal aspects. While it is the lawyer's job to explain the technicalities, the lawyer must do it in a way which will be attractive to the parties whom the client is trying to induce to join in on the deal. Therefore, the lawyer must perform a careful balancing trick of explaining the transaction and its implications in a way which is comprehensible to the audience, of highlighting the advantages and disadvantages of the structure without frightening off the other potential parties to the deal.

This situation involves the lawyer liaising closely with the client so that each of them knows precisely the role the other will be playing. In the case of many presentations, it is not only necessary but also advisable to co-present with others (for example, because of different but complementary areas of expertise or as a way of maintaining the audience's interest in the subject-matter).

The same joint presentation approach may be adopted where a deal has begun to go badly and the lawyer is brought in (whether or not to make a co-presentation with the client) to explain the problems and offer solutions to save the deal. The lawyer must understand the commercial realities which his or her client is facing and come up with solutions which will satisfy both the client and the other parties, if the deal is to be saved.

However, any co-presentation carries with it the danger of the speakers' talks overlapping or leaving important topics entirely untouched. It can sometimes be difficult to know what you should cover when you are the sole presenter; it can be even more difficult to know how to split the responsibilities when there are several presenters. Ensuring the audience get what they are looking for from the presentation by whoever gives it is an important part of the preparation for any presentation.

1.3.5 'Beauty parades' to gain new work

The days of long-term client loyalty are drawing to a close, if they are not entirely over. Many clients want an initial meeting with the lawyer to decide whether or not to give instructions on a particular transaction.

In a typical situation where a beauty parade is called, a client will have a particular transaction in mind. The client will call upon several firms which are able to supply the expertise for which the client is looking to make presentations on their approach to the transaction. Sometimes the potential client will put together a very detailed description of the task and highlight particular issues it wants the lawyers to address. In other cases, the lawyers will receive a general description of the transaction and largely be left to their own devices to decide how to approach the presentation.

With beauty parades, proper preparation is crucial to success. Each lawyer must put himself or herself into the mind of the client to identify precisely what the client is looking for. Although it is dangerous to generalise in this kind of situation, the client is probably not too concerned with receiving confirmation that the lawyer is technically up to the job. Certainly in the case of the larger transactions where beauty parades are involved, the client has been carefully advised by other advisers (for example, merchant banks) on which firms should be called to the beauty parade. Nevertheless, indicating technical expertise is important if the transaction is in some way novel.

Subject to that, the client is usually looking for something, possibly unconnected with the firm's technical expertise, which will convince the client that this is the firm it wishes to appoint to handle the transaction. What each firm can offer which will differentiate it from the others attending the beauty parade will depend on the circumstances. The differentiating factor could be a purely personal feeling that the client can work with the particular firm. It may be connected with the back-up or support the firm can offer in terms of international contacts in the case of a cross-border transaction or extensive computer support in the case of, for example, a multi-plaintiff litigation action. (Identification of the messages the audience hopes to get is a step which must be taken when preparing for any presentation.)

1.3.6   Presenting a training session

In the past decade or so there has been an enormous growth in the provision of legal education beyond the degree and professional examination stage.

The training programme, which may be in-house for the firm, part of a public course organised by a commercial provider of legal education courses or in conjunction with a client, raises a variety of issues. In all cases (as with any presentation), the speaker must decide on the most appropriate method of presenting the information. There are a variety of methods (considered in outline in 3.4.3) which could be adopted, ranging from the talking-head lecture, through discussions and case studies to the use of role-plays or a mixture of all of these.

1.4 SUMMARY

Effective communication skills are essential as a complement to any lawyer's technical ability. These skills can make the difference between a good and an excellent lawyer.

There is an enormous range of activities which may be described as 'presentations' at which communication skills will be exercised. They can cover:

(a) In-house discussions, both face-to-face and over the telephone.

(b) Telephone conversations with outsiders, including clients.

(c) Meetings with clients.

(d) Presentations to get or retain work, whether or not in conjunction with clients.

(e) Formal training sessions.

Chapter Two

The First Step to Effective Communication: Effective Initial Preparation

2.1 THE KEY ELEMENTS OF EFFECTIVE COMMUNICATION

If you are in any situation where you have to communicate a message or information, you will only be able to communicate effectively if you have devoted sufficient time to the three key elements of effective communication:

(a) Effective initial preparation.

(b) Effective structuring of your material.

(c) Effective delivery of the material.

Initial preparation involves researching your topic and the audience to make sure you have collected all the information or data relevant to the presentation. Once you have completed this stage, you should move on to the structuring stage. This is when you decide how to present the information in a way which will communicate your message most effectively to the audience you will be facing. The third and final element of effective communication is the actual delivery of your material to your audience.

This chapter lays down some guidelines for the initial preparation of any presentation and the two succeeding chapters will look at structuring and delivery respectively.

Before looking at the guidelines on initial preparation in 2.4, there is a general explanation (in 2.2) of the need for preparation (which covers all three key elements of effective communication) and (in 2.3) some guidelines on the time to devote to preparing for any presentation.

2.2 THE NEED FOR PREPARATION

It is impossible to present any information in any situation without having prepared beforehand. No one is a natural presenter; everyone has to work at presenting information in an effective way.

You may be able to accept these bald statements easily in relation to formal presentations (such as at in-house training sessions or at beauty parades) but you may have more difficulty accepting them in relation to the other presentations identified in 1.3. Everyone can think of individuals who can be described as 'natural communicators' who seem to be able to explain at a moment's notice, for example, complex issues to clients at meetings without any apparent effort. Such individuals can be likened to swans swimming on a river. All seems grace and elegance as the swans move effortlessly across the water but beneath the surface there is frantic activity as they battle against the current. The 'natural communicator' is able to combine a comprehensive knowledge of his or her subject with perhaps years of experience of dealing with these kinds of situations.

Knowledge of your subject is an essential weapon in your armoury as a good communicator. However, knowledge alone is not enough to ensure a good presentation. You must give thought to the presentation beforehand to ensure it is effective. There is one highly respected, experienced law lecturer at one of the country's most prominent academic institutions who has a plaque on the wall opposite her desk reading:

Fail to prepare, prepare to fail.

Anyone wishing to be a good communicator must keep this warning in mind.

2.3   HOW MUCH TIME SHOULD BE DEVOTED TO PREP-ARATION?

There is no hard-and-fast rule about the time needed for preparation. It depends on the nature of the presentation and the time you have available for preparation.

Clearly, a formal lecture on a new area of law will take longer to prepare than explaining to a new client the issues involved in an area with which you are familiar. Nevertheless, as a broad rule of thumb, the preparation time should be determined by the 'iceberg principle'. Very approximately, an iceberg will have somewhere in the region of only 10 per cent of its mass above water. You should work on the basis that for an hour's worth of presentation, you should devote nine or 10 hours to preparation. Given the work pressures under which many lawyers now operate, this rule of thumb may seem excessive when dealing with a familiar topic. Such a speaker may use his or her existing practical experience as 'credit' against some of the 'iceberg hours'. Even so, practical experience is not a complete substitute for preparation. Time will still need to be spent structuring the presentation in an appropriate way. The guidelines on structuring presentations are given in chapter 3.

Inevitably, the extent of your preparation will be determined by the length of time available. The following paragraphs give guidance on what you can do with preparation times of three weeks, three days and three hours. (These particular periods have been chosen merely for the purposes of illustration.)

2.3.1   Three weeks' preparation time

You will obviously have plenty of time to go through the initial preparation and structuring guidelines set out in this book. This time frame should produce an excellent presentation in which you will deliver your message in an entertaining way which meets the needs of your audience.

The danger of such a relatively long preparation period is that you can over-prepare. You may get bogged down in the initial preparation and, for example, collect far too much information, leaving you confused about how best to structure the information. Furthermore, if you devote this entire period to preparing for the presentation, you will probably become bored with the topic. If you do, your boredom will communicate itself to your audience when you come to make the presentation.

Assuming you have the luxury of time to prepare, use the time sensibly by working on the presentation for only part of the time available and setting sensible deadlines within the preparation period. For example, by the end of the first week you should have completed the initial preparation; by the end of the second week you should have completed the structuring and during the last week you should be honing the delivery of the presentation by the use of rehearsal.

2.3.2 Three days' preparation time

Most lawyers are in the habit of working to deadlines and they are unlikely to change their work practices when preparing for presentations. Despite having weeks' or even months' notice that a presentation has to be given, preparation for the presentation is often left until the last few days before it has to be delivered.

Whatever the reason may be, if you have only a matter of days (which may, in reality, be hours because of other work pressures) in which to prepare for a presentation, the time must be used effectively. You should still follow the guidelines on initial preparation and structuring in this book but the time devoted to each set of guidelines will inevitably be limited.

The problem with time pressure is that you may deny yourself adequate time for all the aspects of preparation. For example, you may rely on your existing knowledge of the subject-matter and not research your topic adequately. Alternatively, you may devote most of the preparation time to ensuring you are technically on top of the subject-matter but overlook the need to structure the presentation in a way which will get your message across effectively to your audience.

The answer is to spend time at the start of the preparation period to timetable a schedule of preparation, allocating appropriate proportions of the time available to the initial preparation, structuring and delivery stages.

2.3.3 Three hours' preparation time

Whether three hours is enough time to prepare a good presentation will depend on the nature of the presentation you are called upon to give. If you are facing the prospect of replacing one of your colleagues who was due to give a formal presentation at an in-house training session on a topic with which you are totally unfamiliar, you may be tempted to feign illness! However, even this situation need not lead to disaster if the possibility of the principal speaker having to drop out at the last minute has been anticipated and you have helped prepare the session. In the time available you should read through your notes on the training session to remind yourself of the issues involved. The task of last-minute preparation in this type of situation can be made easier if the structure for the training session involves audience participation, for example, the use of case studies. While the audience is working its way through the case study, you will have time to familiarise yourself again with the materials.

It is perhaps more likely that you will find yourself faced with a short preparation period when you are called to a meeting unexpectedly. (You should always go to a meeting, no matter how junior you may be, expecting to make some contribution for which you must prepare. You should therefore not find yourself called upon to make some contribution *at* the meeting unexpectedly.)

If you are a trainee solicitor, you may be taken to the meeting with the expectation that you will merely take notes. However, what if, for whatever reason, you are left alone with the clients? While social conversation may not be a problem for you, the client may be more impressed if you can display some knowledge of the transaction or problem on which the client is seeking advice.

Whatever stage in your career you have reached, if you are called to a meeting unexpectedly, you should obtain some background information on the purpose of the meeting. If you have been called to a meeting because a point which falls within your particular area of expertise has arisen, you should extract from the colleague who has summoned you to the meeting as much relevant information about the client and his or her problem as the time allows. You should also make sure that you give yourself time to order your thoughts so as to present your points in a logical way. Naturally, everyone wishes to avoid the embarrassment faced by a young barrister who, having taken over a brief from a colleague taken suddenly ill, announced to the court that he was acting for the plaintiff in the action only to be told by the judge that he was acting for the defendant.

2.4 THE STAGES OF INITIAL PREPARATION

There are seven questions you must always ask when embarking on the initial preparation stage for *any* presentation. These questions are:

(a) What are the objectives of the presentation?

(b) Who will be in the audience?

(c) What is the timing of the presentation?

(d) What research do I need to do for the presentation?

(e) What will be the venue for the presentation?

(f) What documentation, if any, do I need to prepare for the presentation?

(g) What visual aids, if any, do I need to prepare for the presentation?

These seven questions must be asked and answered whether you have three hours or three weeks to prepare for the presentation. The time available and/or the nature of the presentation will determine the answers to some of these questions but this does not mean they should not be asked. Once answered, they will give you the information you need to move on to the structuring stage and will make that stage much easier (by making some of the necessary decisions inevitable).

The issues to be addressed when considering each of these seven questions are set out in 2.4.1 to 2.4.7.

2.4.1   What are the objectives of the presentation?

Every presentation, no matter how long or short it may be, no matter how formal or informal it may be, has a purpose or objective. It is your task to identify what that objective is. It could be to explain the results of some research you have carried out for your principal. It could be to explain to your client the range of possible alternative solutions to his or her problem and to give advice on the approach you consider should be taken. It could be to explain your client's position to the 'other side' and then to embark on a negotiation to reach a compromise acceptable to both sides. It could be to explain a complex legal issue at an in-house training session.

While it should be easy to identify in a sentence or two the principal objective of most, if not all, presentations, that is not the end of the objective identification stage. All you have done so far is to identify the broad purpose of the presentation. You must then go on to identify your personal objective. You must identify the message you want your audience to take away with them from the presentation. If the purpose of the presentation is to offer a client a suggested solution to a particular problem, you must have clear in your own mind which solution you intend recommending. If you are explaining a complex legal issue at a training session, you must decide whether your objective is to give the audience all the information they need to deal with the problem if it arises in practice, or merely highlight the circumstances in which it can arise so that they know when to contact an expert (i.e., you) for specific advice.

Linked with identifying your own objective for the presentation, you should be clear in your own mind why you, rather than anyone else, is giving the presentation. Often this is not an issue because, for example, you are the lawyer dealing with this particular client's affairs. It is, however, a crucial point for many formal presentations, such as lectures or beauty parades. In the case of lectures, there may be any number of people who are suitably qualified to give the talk; many of them may be sitting in your audience. The answer may be that you are perceived by the organiser of the lecture to have the necessary technical and/or practical experience to make anything you have to say on the topic worthwhile to hear. You may know this but does your audience? As will be explained in chapter 3, it is important to establish your credibility with your audience as quickly as possible. In the case of beauty parades, the likelihood is that you will be the person in charge of work, assuming your firm is chosen. This will need to be explained to the prospective client.

You should never forget there are two sides to the presentation equation, the presenter *and* the audience. The audience has expectations of what they will get from the presentation and you should try to anticipate what they may be.

Whatever the objective of the presentation may be, you should ensure that throughout your preparation for the presentation you bear the objective in mind. If you do, you will ensure that that objective is achieved.

2.4.2 Who will be in the audience?

It will be impossible to communicate your message effectively to your audience if you do not know anything about them. The issues you should bear in mind are:

(a) How many people will be in your audience? The approach you adopt for delivering the information will differ depending on whether the audience will be made up of one, 10 or 100. If the presentation is to be delivered one-to-one, the style you adopt will be that of a conversation. If the audience is relatively small (say, 10 or fewer) you may want the audience to participate in a discussion. For larger audiences, particularly if you are the only speaker, you will have little alternative but to adopt a formal lecturing approach.

(b) Are you acquainted with the people in the audience? If the presentation is to an existing client with whom you get on well or to your colleagues within the firm or organisation, you can probably adopt a relatively relaxed approach. If the audience is made up of strangers, a more formal style may be more appropriate.

(c)   What is the audience's existing level of knowledge of the topic you will be covering? If you do not know the answer to this question, you will not be able to pitch your presentation at a level which they will find helpful. If you pitch it too low, the audience will probably imagine you are displaying the full extent of your knowledge and so hold you in contempt. If you pitch it too high, the audience may be impressed by your grasp of the subject but find what you say incomprehensible and so get no value from the presentation.

(d)   What if the audience is a 'mixed-ability' group? One of the most difficult problems faced by any presenter is that of coping with an audience made up of individuals with different levels of knowledge of the subject-matter. There are a number of ways to approach this problem. The most common is to find the median level of knowledge and let that determine the pitch of your presentation. The problem with such an approach is that the least knowledgeable members of your audience will be confused and the most knowledgeable will be bored. An alternative, but not easy to achieve, is to try to pitch your presentation in a way which will mean that every member of your audience derives some benefit. To put this point into context, imagine you have been called upon to explain the approach to a particular transaction which your firm recommends to its clients. You discover the audience will be a mixture of trainee solicitors, assistant solicitors and partners. Were you to explain the deal for the benefit only of the assistant solicitors, you would probably find the trainees doodling on their notepads and the partners leaving the room, muttering that they had better ways of spending their time. However, you could open the presentation with a short and simple explanation of the way the transaction is structured. This would mean the trainee solicitors would understand the purpose of such transactions and you are maximising the chances of them being able to understand the more detailed points you intend covering later. It is true that the assistant solicitors and the partners will be hearing information they already know but, within reason, everyone likes reassurance of their own technical or practical knowledge. Having laid this foundation, you can then move on to consider the transaction at a level which the assistant solicitors will find acceptable. While this may be too advanced for some of the trainees, if you have laid the foundations well, most will probably pick up the key points you are making. Unfortunately, the senior end of your audience, the partners, will still feel they are gaining nothing from the presentation. Therefore, the third element of your presentation should be to include high-powered points which are of interest to that section of your audience. To maintain the interest of your audience it is probably better to mix the points aimed at the assistant solicitors and those aimed at partners, rather than leaving the points for the partners until the very end. This approach of mixing the points may be very beneficial to the assistant solicitors. They will probably find it easier to understand the high-powered points if they are linked with points they understand rather than delivered in isolation.

(e) What is the age range of your audience? What is the male-female mix? What is the racial mix of your audience? The make-up of your audience should be borne in mind so as to ensure you avoid the risk of giving offence to any group or individual.

(f) Are you talking to a lay or qualified audience? The latter will probably have no difficulty dealing with technical language or jargon whereas the former probably will. The key point is to adjust your style of presentation to suit the level of understanding of your audience. Using case names as a shorthand when explaining relevant legal issues to a criminal client will not be helpful. Conversely, failing to use the relevant technical jargon when talking to your commercial clients may lead them to doubt your knowledge of their business.

(g) What attitude will the audience have towards you? Will they be sympathetic, neutral or antagonistic? Clients who are relying on you to give them guidance on how to extract themselves from a difficult situation will be very attentive. However, they may listen to your presentation without exercising their critical faculties. This could mean they simply accept everything you say without challenging a point which, unbeknownst to you, may not in fact apply in their case. An audience of trainee solicitors at an in-house presentation on the way the firm's time-recording system works may find the subject-matter less than gripping. It will be up to the presenter to engage their interest by using some of the techniques for audience participation explained in chapter 3. If the purpose of the presentation is to explain why a transaction has gone wrong or to explain your client's position to the other side in a negotiation, the audience will inevitably be predisposed against your arguments. You will have to marshal your thoughts so as to give your arguments maximum strength.

(h)   What is the linguistic ability of your audience? In these days of a multiracial society in this country, many lawyers have to advise clients for whom English is not their first language. The international nature of commerce means that this issue is of relevance to virtually all lawyers irrespective of the nature of their practices. This adds a further complication to the factors identified in the preceding paragraphs. It may be possible for you to find out the audience's level of language and then to pitch your use of English at their level. If in doubt about the level of the client's knowledge of English, the safest approach is to keep the presentation as simple as possible and to back the presentation up with a written document which the client will be able to study later, possibly with the benefit of a dictionary.

(i)   Last but by no means least, you must find out what the audience expect to get from the presentation. To what extent do their expectations match with your objectives? If they are different, you will have to decide whether you need to adjust your objectives or to explain to the audience that their expectations are incorrect. Come what may, you must ensure, so far as possible, that there is a meeting of minds at the presentation.

For many presentations you will give (for example, to existing clients) you will know the answers to all these questions. If you are in a position where you do not know the answer to any one or more of them, you must always seek out the answers at this initial stage of preparing for the presentation. If you are preparing for an initial meeting with a new client, you may be able to get some, if not all, of the answers from the client when arranging the meeting or from a third party (such as the colleague who introduced you to the client). If it is difficult to get answers to all of these questions beforehand, you should be prepared to be flexible when you make the presentation.

It may be particularly difficult to get answers to these questions when you are presenting a formal lecture at a public conference because you will have no direct contact with the audience. Even in that case, you can get some information from the delegate lists which will usually give the name of each delegate and their firm or organisation as well as, possibly, their status within their firm or organisation.

2.4.3   What is the timing of the presentation?

There are two aspects to this question:

(a)   When in the day will you be making your presentation?

(b)   How long will your presentation be?

Dealing with the timing of the presentation first, it should go without saying that there are certain times of the day when your audience is likely to be more receptive to a presentation than at others. The audience will be able to take on board more complex information if a presentation is early in the morning than they will if it is immediately after lunch or late in the day. Even so, a presentation at a client meeting organised for 5.00 p.m. will probably have a more attentive audience than a similar presentation at the same time which is the final talk in a day-long conference. This point is explained in more detail in chapter 3 where the concentration level of typical audiences is explained.

The second factor on timing is the length of your presentation. If you have been allocated a fixed period, you should make sure you cover the topic in the time available. Clearly, the time available may determine a variety of aspects of your approach to the presentation including the level of detail you go into and the method of presentation you adopt.

2.4.4   What research do I need to do for the presentation?

Once you have identified the objectives of the presentation and have a clear knowledge of the audience, you will be in a position to determine the extent to which you need to engage in research in preparation for the presentation.

This book is not intended to be a treatise on legal research methods. Therefore, it is assumed that you will be able to identify the legal issues involved in a presentation and to take advantage of whatever legal research tools may be available to you to complete this aspect of the preparation stage.

However, it is always worthwhile to consider whether other research is necessary. You may have researched the background of the client prior to a meeting with the client but, particularly in the case of commercial clients, are you able to find out anything about your client's competitors? What do you know about the client's business sector generally? If you are explaining your firm's approach to a particular type of transaction at an in-house training session, do you know the approach adopted by your competitors? If their approach differs, do you know why this is? How will you justify your firm's approach as being the better approach?

When dealing with this stage of the preparation, you will obviously engage in 'active' research on questions which you wish to cover in the presentation to which you do not know the answer. However, the benefit of 'passive' research (that is to say, drawing on your existing technical and practical knowledge) should not be overlooked. Whoever your audience may be, they will find it helpful to have technical points put into a practical context. Therefore, if you could draw on your own experience to give illustrations, this will give added depth and colour to the presentation. It will be a tremendous aid to maintaining the audience's concentration. It will help the audience understand and remember the information you are giving to them.

2.4.5   What will be the venue for the presentation?

The nature of the presentation and the size of the audience will determine the venue for the presentation. You should, nevertheless, give thought to the venue, considering not only its physical construction but also the layout of the venue and the equipment available.

If you are attending a meeting, you and the other participants are likely to be sitting around a table. Your position in relation to your audience can have an impact on the effectiveness of the presentation. Can they all see you? Do you have your back to any of them? If the presentation is more formal, such as a lecture or beauty parade, the seating of the audience remains important. Is it appropriate for you and the audience to sit round a table? Should you stand and the audience sit? Should you provide the audience only with chairs or with tables as well? Should the seats be in a U-shape, in 'classroom' style (i.e., with tables and chairs in rows stretching to the back of the room) or in 'theatre' style (rows of chairs alone stretching to the back of the room)?

What do you know of the construction of the room? Are the sightlines good from every part of the room or are they blocked (for example, by roof support pillars)? How easy will it be for your audience to get to and from the venue? Do you need to supply them with maps? Where are the room's entrances and exits? Will the room be noisy?

Do you know what equipment will be available in the room? If you wish to use some form of visual aid, it would be a disaster to discover that the necessary equipment was not available or that the room was not suitable for the particular technology you intended using.

In big rooms or rooms with poor acoustics, it may be necessary to consider some kind of amplification system. Is this available or will it have to be organised?

These problems and other logistical issues are covered in chapter 6.

2.4.6 What documentation, if any, do I need to prepare for the presentation?

The final stage of your initial preparation for a presentation is to consider the use you intend making of presentation aids. This section will look at the factors to take into account when considering what documents, if any, you need to prepare. Paragraph 2.4.7 will look at the need for visual aids.

The documents you can prepare can be divided into two categories:

(a)   The documents you prepare for your own benefit.

(b)   The documents you prepare for the benefit of your audience.

Chapter 5 examines in some detail the preparation of documentation to support any presentation. This section of this chapter will help you to decide whether you *need* any supporting documents.

Irrespective of the length of the presentation and also irrespective of your familiarity with the subject-matter, it is worthwhile preparing some form of notes for your own use to ensure that you cover the points you wish to get across in a sensible order. In the heat of the moment of the presentation, there is always the risk of you losing your train of thought no matter how well you have prepared. A set of notes will help you get back on track.

How detailed the notes need to be will depend on the nature of the presentation and your familiarity with the detail of the topic. Chapter 5 contains guidance on preparing a set of notes which will help to maximise the impact of your presentation. In brief, the advice that chapter contains is to prepare a set of notes which will help you deliver your presentation in a natural, conversational tone.

What documents you need to prepare to help the audience will depend on the nature of the presentation. Documents should be sent to the audience *before* the presentation if they need to have knowledge of the subject-matter of the presentation beforehand in order to get the maximum benefit.

If you are giving a formal presentation, you can issue an outline of your talk in the form of a series of bullet points or outline notes. This will help your audience understand the structure of your presentation and help them to put any notes they may make of your presentation into the appropriate context.

After the presentation you may wish to distribute a 'paper' containing the detail of your presentation. It can contain any information you want the audience to take away with them but which you had insufficient time to cover. It can confirm advice given or agreement reached at a meeting.

2.4.7 What visual aids, if any, do I need to prepare for the presentation?

Chapter 5 considers the benefits of having visual aids as well as examining the advantages and disadvantages of the different types of visual aid.

At this stage in your preparation for the presentation, you will know what equipment, if any, is available to help you with your presentation (see 2.4.5). You should now decide whether the presentation needs to be supported by the use of visual aids.

One of the principal uses of visual aids is to help maintain the audience's attention and concentration. Therefore, visual aids are probably essential for long presentations and could be useful even for short ones.

As a simple rule of thumb, in *any* presentation involving something which can more easily be understood if it is seen, visual aids should be used, irrespective of the length or nature of the presentation. For example, if the purpose of the presentation is to explain the structure of a transaction, it will almost always be easier to draw the structure.

Visual aids need not only be used at formal sessions. They can be extremely useful at client meetings, albeit that in those circumstances you may be using relatively simple 'technology', such as flip charts rather than overhead projectors or slide projectors.

2.5 SUMMARY

Once you have worked your way through the guidelines in this chapter, you will have completed your initial preparation for the presentation. You should have:

(a) A clear idea of the purpose of the talk.

(b) An understanding of the audience and its needs and interests.

(c) A knowledge of the time of day at which you will be speaking and the length of time for which you will be speaking.

(d) Completed your researches on all matters which are of relevance to the presentation.

(e) Be aware of the venue for the presentation.

(f)   Have decided upon the nature of any documentation you
need to prepare (for the benefit of both yourself and the audience) in
support of the presentation.

(g)   A clear idea of whether you will use visual aids and, if so,
which format for visual aids you will use.

The result of all this effort will be a mass of information, probably
covering many sheets of paper. While you may use most, if not all, of
this information in your presentation, you are still only part of the
way through preparing the presentation. The next stage is to put the
information into an order which will ensure you achieve the
objectives you have identified and give your audience what they are
looking for. Guidance on structuring your presentation is given in
chapter 3.

Chapter Three

The Second Step to Effective Communication: Effective Structuring of the Presentation

3.1 INTRODUCTION

Once you have completed the initial preparation stage, you should have in your possession a mass of information. You are now ready to move on to the structuring stage. You may find that once you have completed the initial preparation stage, to a greater or lesser extent, some of the structuring decisions will already have been made. This chapter gives guidelines on how to structure your presentation in a way which will help you maximise the impact of your presentation. Put simply, you should structure your presentation into three parts:

(a)   The introduction in which you tell your audience in outline what they will hear.

(b)   The main body of your talk in which you will develop your theme.

(c)   The conclusion in which you will summarise what the audience have heard and give them the key message you wish them to take away.

Needless to say, this book is not advocating that in any presentation you should repeat *exactly* the same information three times. This book advocates this three-stage approach because, using the techniques described in 3.3 below for introducing your presentation, you will be able to put the principal subject-matter of your talk into context for the audience. They will be prepared to absorb the information and understand your perception of how the information you are about to present relates to them. Having developed your theme in the main body of your talk (the techniques are described in 3.4), in your conclusion you will draw together the strands of your presentation and highlight whatever the key message may be. How you should do this is explained in 3.5.

This three-stage approach (sometimes called the 'Golden Three') is based on the principle that if you hear a proposition once you may not fully understand it and are therefore unlikely either to believe or remember it. If you hear it a second time, any queries may be answered and you will have sufficient information to be able to decide whether you agree with the point. The third time you hear the same item of information you should understand it and therefore the repetition will help you remember the point. Whether you agree with the point and (if appropriate) act upon it will depend on the persuasiveness of the speaker.

3.2 AN ILLUSTRATION FROM THE COMMUNICATIONS INDUSTRY AND ITS GENERAL APPLICATION

It may be helpful to put the guidelines on structuring a presentation which are set out in the succeeding paragraphs into a practical context with which you are familiar. Each day anyone with access to a television can watch an illustration of effective communication at its best by watching the television news programmes. Both the BBC's 'Nine O'Clock News' and ITN's 'News at Ten' illustrate perfectly the techniques for delivering often complex messages to a widely differing audience in an effective and memorable way.

While the detailed structure of the presentation differs (in that the 'News At Ten' team has to cope with the problem of the advertising break halfway through the programme), the overall structure for the two programmes is identical. In the case of each programme, the presentation has:

(a)   An introduction, when the main news items are summarised in a sentence or phrase between musical cords (the BBC) or the chimes of Big Ben (ITN).

(b)   A 'main body' when the main items are examined in more detail in relatively short segments (usually not lasting more than 5 minutes each).

(c)   A conclusion, when the main stories are summarised again in a phrase or sentence.

Looking at the presentation in more detail:

(a)   Both programmes adopt the approach of covering a number of completely separate stories. This will mean that the audience is unlikely to get bored because no one story goes on for too long. By covering a range of different stories, there is likely to be something in the bulletin which will interest virtually everyone watching. The entire audience, therefore, goes away with something of benefit to them.

(b)   Both programmes use the technique of having more than one presenter. Usually 'News at Ten' has two principal newscasters delivering alternate items (or introducing a third reporter to perform this task). The 'Nine O'Clock News' usually has a single principal newscaster but he or she always introduces other reporters to cover some of the items in the bulletin. This technique ensures that the audience does not get bored with one person.

(c)   Both programmes make very heavy use of visual aids either in the form of filmed reports or the use of graphics.

(d)   'News at Ten' has to cope with the advertising break halfway through the bulletin. The team takes advantage of the break to repeat the short introductory descriptions of the main stories which will be considered in the second half. They also often introduce some form of appealing 'human interest' story (of the 'Four year old saves Father Christmas' variety).

The presentations you are likely to be giving are unlikely to have the interest level of a news bulletin. Nevertheless, the *techniques* used by these news programmes can apply irrespective of the subject-matter of the presentation.

3.3   THE INTRODUCTION

3.3.1   How long should the introduction be?

The length of the introduction will depend on the nature of the presentation. You should probably devote not less than 5 per cent and not more than 15 per cent of the total length of the presentation to this stage. If the presentation is a telephone call to your client to obtain information, your introduction will consist of you identifying yourself, explaining briefly the nature of the information you are seeking and the reason why you need it. If the presentation is more formal, the points to be covered in the introduction are set out in 3.3.2.

3.3.2   What should the introduction contain?

There are a variety of points to be considered when deciding how to phrase and structure your introduction. The circumstances of the presentation will determine how you deal with certain of the points but all should at least be considered. For the sake of simplicity, the points listed below are aimed principally at a *formal* presentation (whether at a lecture or a beauty parade). Obviously, some of the points will not be relevant to more informal presentations over the telephone or at client meetings.

Why should the audience listen to the presenter?

You need to introduce yourself and establish your credibility with your audience as soon as possible. A brief description of your status within your organisation and practical experience will suffice for most of the formal presentations made by lawyers. If you are part of a team of speakers, there may be a chairman who will introduce you. It is, nevertheless, always advisable to have agreed in advance how you will be described.

By giving some indication of your practical experience, you will help the audience understand why you, rather than anyone else, are giving the presentation. If you are giving a talk on government privatisations and you have recently led a team which dealt with such a transaction, referring to this (within the bounds of professional confidentiality) will immediately give the audience reason to have confidence in your knowledge of the subject. Similarly, suppose you are leading your firm's team at a beauty parade before a building society when you are seeking to persuade them to appoint you to their panel of solicitors. Describing your experience as the head of the conveyancing department and prime mover in the introduction of a computerised conveyancing system will give added weight to the points you make.

Needless to say, it is almost certainly counter-productive to go over the top with a detailed description of your personal CV.

Once you have established your credibility, you may feel that you wish to break the ice between you and the audience by introducing some humour into your presentation. While any audience will regard an *amusing* speaker as an added bonus, care must be taken when trying to be funny. Setting aside the possibility of the subject-matter of the joke causing offence, you may find your attempt at humour gets the presentation off to a bad start. This will happen if the joke you choose has no relevance to the subject-matter of your presentation or if the audience does not find the joke amusing. Save for those fortunate individuals who are naturally funny, the better approach is probably to break the ice with the audience by introducing a relevant anecdote from your personal experience. If it is carefully chosen, it will reveal to the audience that you have a practical understanding of the topic you will be covering and hopefully will be something to which members of the audience can themselves relate. In a few short sentences you may have managed to create an immediate bond with the audience.

What topics will the speaker cover?

The audience should have an idea of the title of the presentation (particularly if it is a formal lecture) and certainly will have an idea of the topics they expect to be covered. There is, however, the danger that despite the effort you have put into the initial preparation stage, for some of the audience at least, their expectations and your intentions do not match. You should, therefore, explain to the audience as soon as possible what you will be covering and, in outline, how you intend covering it. At this stage you should highlight (but only very briefly) the key points you will be developing when you come on to the main body of your talk.

Why does the audience need to know the information the speaker will be presenting?

Merely telling the audience that you will be covering a particular topic does not of itself give them any reason to listen to the presentation. You should, therefore, identify your perception of their need to listen to you. In most cases, the audience will be aware of their own need. However, there are circumstances when this is not the case, for example, where you are explaining the impact of new legislation or a recently decided case. Accordingly, you should plant in the audience's minds the message you are trying to get across and give them some reason for listening to you. You should take pains to phrase this section of the introduction in a way which will make the audience *want* to hear what you have to say.

How much of the topic will the speaker cover?

If it is not self-evident from the title or subject-matter of your presentation how much detail you will be going into, you should make this clear at the outset. If time pressures mean that you are only able to highlight a few key points of a very broad topic, you should tell the audience in advance. Failure to do so may mean that some of the audience will feel short-changed. If you are forced by circumstances to omit areas you would have liked to cover, you may have decided to put that information into a handout. You should tell the audience this.

What will the audience get from the presentation?

Although this to some extent overlaps with the first question (why should the audience listen to the presenter?) both the speaker and the audience need to be clear about the outcome of the presentation.

What are the rules of this presentation?

Finally, you should give the audience instructions on their behaviour. If you have prepared documentation and issued it to the audience, how should they use it? By explaining this at the outset you minimise the risk of the audience flicking through the materials to find out their purpose while you are speaking. If you are intending to issue documentation *after* the presentation is over, what documentation will they receive? The audience will appreciate you telling them that they can concentrate on what you are saying rather than, for example, copying the text of your overhead projector slides or scribbling notes of your talk because they will receive copies of those slides or a full paper afterwards.

If you intend to get the audience to do something (such as break up into discussion groups, consider a case study or take part in role-plays), you should give them notice. Depending on the nature of the audience participation, you may have decided to issue information about the activities in advance of the presentation. If that is the case, at this stage you should explain the practicalities of their participation.

Hopefully, your presentation will be sufficiently thought-provoking to induce your audience to ask questions. Are you willing to take any such questions during the presentation or would you prefer to take them all at the end? Members of small audiences are more likely to ask questions during the presentation than members of large audiences. There are dangers in taking questions *during* the presentation. Considering and answering the questions will inevitably break your chain of thought. It can cause confusion among the rest of the audience, especially if the question anticipates a point you were intending to cover later in the presentation. In the latter circumstance, if you answer the question, you will have to deviate from your planned, logical order. Doing so carries with it the risk that everyone other than the questioner will have insufficient knowledge of the topic to be able to see how the point you are making fits into the overall picture. The techniques for handling questions are dealt with in more detail in chapter 6.

3.4   THE MAIN BODY OF THE PRESENTATION

3.4.1   How long should the main body be?

Inevitably, you will devote the bulk of your presentation to developing your main theme or themes. You are likely to devote upwards of 75 per cent of the time available to this section of the presentation.

3.4.2   What should be included in the main body of the presentation?

The answer to this question is simple and obvious: whatever information or message you want to get across to the audience. Simple though this answer may be, it is not very helpful. Therefore, the following paragraphs give guidance on structuring this section of the presentation.

The average person's attention span and thinking speed

Research studies have shown that most people can concentrate on a single topic for only 10 or 11 minutes. Research has also been conducted into the level of attention of the average member of an audience during a typical lecture lasting 45 minutes. A rough approximation of the results of the research is set out in the graph in figure 3.1.

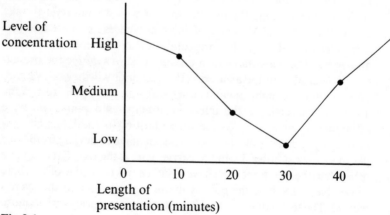

Fig 3.1

The research which has been done on the average person's thinking speed has shown that most people think at a rate of 400–600 words per minute whereas, with rare exceptions, most people talk at the rate of 150–200 words per minute. This rate often falls when the speaker is presenting at a formal lecture and is anxious to avoid gabbling.

How can you use these research results?

(a)   The minds of the members of the audience will wander if you cover the same topic for more than 10 minutes or so. Therefore, the presentation should be broken up into sections. (This is examined in more detail later in 3.4.2.)

(b)   The audience's attention will be high at the beginning of the presentation, will dip in the middle, *assuming you take no steps to re-engage the audience's attention earlier*, but will rise at the end. You should, therefore, at the very least ensure that key messages are delivered at the beginning and end of the presentation (using the 'Golden Three' approach). The methods which can be used to *prevent* the audience's attention dipping during the presentation are examined later in 3.4.2.

(c)   You should assume that everyone in the audience is thinking quicker than you are speaking. Accordingly, some or all of the audience will be thinking about something else while you are presenting. To prevent their minds wandering, you have to devise ways of engaging their attention.

(d)   Although the research referred to above concentrated on attention spans within lectures, the same broad principle applies to, for example, day-long courses. The audience is likely to be able to concentrate best at the beginning and end of the day. Therefore, in the duller central sections of the day, consideration should be given to using more lively methods of presentation which are, again, described below.

Structuring the main body of the talk

In the main body of your presentation you will be communicating your message or information. Having completed the initial preparation stage, you will have a mass of information which you should now arrange into a logical order for delivery to the audience. This raises two issues:

(a)   Which items should be included in the presentation?

(b)   In what order should those items be delivered?

Much of the data you will have collected during the initial preparation stage will be background information (such as details about the audience). This merely needs to be taken into account when deciding on the pitch of the presentation. The balance of the data you have collected can probably be divided into three categories:

(a)   Important information which must be explained to the audience.

(b)   Useful information which could be explained to the audience if there is time but which should probably be set out in a handout for the audience to take away.

(c)   Background information which at most could be dealt with *very briefly* in the presentation and is probably best put into a handout or possibly omitted altogether.

With these three categories in mind, you should be able to rank each item of information you have collected. To put this into a practical example, suppose you have been asked to explain the succession consequences of someone dying intestate. The important points to cover are an explanation of the intestacy rules and the procedure to be followed when applying for letters of adminstration of the intestate's estate. Depending on the circumstances, it will probably not be appropriate to go into details on the hotchpot rules in the presentation; it might be useful to prepare a handout giving details of these rules for your audience to take away. If the presentation is to be delivered to the beneficiaries of an intestate deceased, there is clearly no point explaining the administration advantages which could have been gained had the deceased made a will.

Once you have decided, in broad terms, which points are going to be delivered to the audience and the method of delivery (that is to say, whether you explain the points orally or put the points into a handout), the next step is to decide the order in which to deal with the points.

If you are explaining a procedure, the procedure itself may determine the order for dealing with the issue. Continuing with the illustration above, when you are dealing with the procedure for applying for letters of administration, it would be illogical to deal with the procedure for selling assets before explaining the procedure which has to be followed to obtain the grant.

If the subject-matter does not decide the order in which points should be covered you are faced with a broad range of options. If you decide there are five key points you wish to get across, you can rank them in order of importance. If number one is the most important and number five is the least important, what is the best order to follow? If you start with point number one (the most important), every point you make thereafter is an anti-climax. If you start with point number five and work your way up through the order, you are finishing on a high note but the audience may be bored by your early points. They may not, therefore, engage their minds when you deliver you *pièce de résistance*. One work on presentation skills (*Handbook of Management Skills* edited by Dorothy M. Stewart Gower Publishing) recommends following the advice of the ancient Greek masters of oratory. If you follow their approach you will start the main body of your presentation with *point number two* (your second best point), follow it with points numbers three, four and five and finish with point number one. This approach has the benefit of starting the presentation on a relatively high note and ending it on the issue of greatest importance.

Once you have a logical order for your presentation, you will then go on to develop your theme in relation to each point. The level of detail will depend on the time available. However, come what may, you should bear in mind the audience's collective attention span (see above). Accordingly, you should aim to deal with each key point in less than 10 minutes. Alternatively, you could think about introducing some kind of break or change of approach into your presentation at the end of each 10-minute section. More detailed guidance on how to stage the presentation is given in 3.4.2.

This book is not advocating that at the end of each 10-minute section of the presentation there should necessarily be a complete change of direction. Rather, at that point in the presentation, something should be done to attract the audience's attention and to help them maintain their concentration levels. It may be that the nature of the presentation means you can indeed achieve this aim by a change of direction. This will be the case, for example, if the presentation is on the tax rules applicable to trusts. In that case, it may be possible to structure the main body of the presentation so that separate 10-minute sections are devoted to considering the liabilities which can arise in relation to inheritance tax, capital gains tax and income tax. If the subject-matter does not lend itself to this kind of break, you should nevertheless consider breaking up the presentation at regular intervals. A simple technique would be to use a visual aid or to ask the audience a question. A more complicated technique would be to get the audience to do something, such as examine a case study or act out a role-play.

The important point is to ensure you structure your presentation in a way which will minimise the risk of the audience letting their minds wander, thus losing the thread of your argument and so becoming bored and inattentive. The concept of the 10-minute sections is a guideline only. It could be counter-productive to structure your talk so that exactly at the end of each 10-minute section some supposedly attention-grabbing device is introduced. The 10-minute section concept should merely be borne in mind so as to avoid allowing any one section to run on in an unbroken, unenlivened way for too long.

Methods of maintaining the audience's interest

Suppose a seamless presentation on a complex topic is delivered in a dull monotone by an apparently emotionless speaker without the use of any presentation aids. What will be the effect on the audience? They will be reduced to a group of fidgeting, doodling, clock-watchers who are taking nothing in but merely waiting for the torture to end. Some of the problems envisaged in that scenario will be covered in chapter 4 (dealing with delivery). However, the possible methods of engaging the audience's attention (and so ensuring that their collective concentration level is high) are set out in this section. These are:

(a) Use visual aids. These may be flip charts, overhead projector slides, 35 mm slides and videos (whether videoing the participants carrying out some activity or using professionally produced training videos). The mere use of a visual aid, whatever type it may be, will attract the audience's attention. If the visual aid is used badly their attention will slip after a few seconds; if it is used well, it can maintain their attention for far longer.

(b) Use the technique of 'peeping'. This involves giving the audience something to look forward to. It is a technique commonly used on television news programmes (such as when the 'News at Ten' newscaster summarises the main stories to be covered after the break at the end of the first half of the programme). If the audience is made to believe there is something of interest to them coming shortly in the presentation, they will concentrate on the presentation (even before the interesting point is reached) out of concern that they may miss the point.

(c) Get the audience involved. This could take the form of illustrating a technical point with a practical anecdote. If the audience understand how the points you are making work in practice they will find a technical talk more useful. Injecting humour is an effective attention-grabber provided the audience does become involved by laughing. The humour can come from what you say or from what the audience sees. A joke on a visual aid can be just as funny as a joke you tell but either can be disastrous if they fall flat. The best way of maintaining the audience's attention is by getting them to do something (for example, answering a question you have posed or carrying out a role-play). The various alternative ways of running a training programme are considered in paragraph 3.4.3 below.

(d) Use breaks. If the presentation is likely to last a long time (for example, for more than one hour), it is advisable to introduce a break after, say, 45 minutes. The break could be inactive in the sense that it simply gives the audience an opportunity to stretch their legs.

Alternatively, it could be active in the sense that the presenter, for example, agrees to take questions for a few minutes. If the presentation is going to last for a half day or a full day, there will be obvious natural breaks (for coffee, lunch and tea). However, these will only break the day into four segments which are likely to be 90 minutes long. Short breaks (probably no longer than five minutes) should be introduced halfway through each of the four segments.

(e)   Use more than one presenter. Merely hearing a different voice will attract the audience's attention but this device should be used with care. There must be a valid reason why one presenter has finished and the next has begun. This is easier to justify where there are several separate topics to be covered (for example, where the tax and company law aspects of a particular transaction will be examined) than where the presentation is on a single topic. Even if the presentation is on a single topic (for example, the procedure to be followed when one company is trying to take over another), the use of two speakers can be very effective. Each could describe the stages in the transaction from the perspectives of the bidder company and target company respectively.

3.4.3   Presentation methods

There have been passing references throughout the text to the various methods which can be adopted to get your message across to the audience. In this section, the benefits and disadvantages of the main methods are examined. However, this book is intended to be an introduction to the topic. It does not attempt to explain any of the theories on how human beings learn or remember information. For that information the reader is referred to the standards texts on educational theory. Having said that, there is one simple educational theory which is worth bearing in mind and can be summarised as follows:

I hear   I forget

I see   I remember

I do   I understand

The talking-head approach

This involves the presenter standing in front of the audience and delivering a speech. From the presenter's viewpoint, this is a highly effective way of delivering the information to the audience. The presenter is in total control, assuming that he or she either takes no questions during the presentation or carefully controls queries. He or she can be certain that the points in the presentation will be covered in the carefully considered sequence he or she decided upon when preparing the presentation. From the audience's viewpoint, such a method of delivery is the least effective way of ensuring they will understand and retain the subject-matter of the presentation. This method of presentation, therefore, falls within the first tenet of the educational theory.

At the very least, the presenter should try to bring the presentation within the second of the educational theory's tenets by the use of visual aids (see chapter 5).

When is the talking-head approach appropriate? If a sole presenter is dealing with a relatively large audience (say, 25 or more) it is almost certainly not realistic for him or her to use any of the more participative methods described below, other than the questioning technique. Irrespective of the size of the audience, this technique will probably be the most sensible to use if the presentation is very short, lasting not more than, say, 10 minutes. In such a case there is not likely to be enough time to do anything participative which is of real benefit.

It is also sensible to use this technique if the presenter has to get across a lot of detailed information (for example, on a degree course) in a short time.

Blanket or pinpoint questioning

This technique involves the presenter throwing questions at the audience with those questions either addressed to the audience as a whole (blanket questioning) or to particular individuals (pinpoint questioning).

This technique is sometimes used merely to maintain the audience's level of concentration. However, it does also have educational value in that it can satisfy the third tenet of the educational theory (I do, I understand). This requires each question to be phrased carefully. The member of the audience who answers it will have to use the information he or she has gained from the presentation to answer the problem contained in the question.

This approach can be stretching so far as the audience is concerned but, to be effective, the audience must have an understanding of the subject-matter. If the presentation you are preparing is on a complex topic, it is probably unrealistic to hope to be able to use this technique, save where you are trying to test your audience's *basic* understanding.

Discussion groups

As the title makes clear, this technique involves the audience (whether as a whole if the numbers are small or in groups where the numbers are larger) discussing a particular issue or issues. On the face of it, this method does not involve a presentation at all; you simply give the issue to the group and let them range over the issue as they think fit. Such a 'hands-off' approach could be disastrous both in terms of reaching *any* conclusion (let alone the one you are seeking) and in terms of the group covering all the aspects of the issue you wish them to examine.

Therefore, you should first decide whether the circumstances justify the use of this technique. It is obviously completely inappropriate if you are trying to explain some technical point with which the group is unfamiliar. Conversely, it is wholly appropriate if the purpose of the session is for the audience to decide collectively the solution to a problem or to reach some strategic decision. It would be foolish in those circumstances not to give the group some guidance. Therefore, it is probably advisable for you to give a brief introductory (talking-head) presentation.

This approach has the enormous benefit of ensuring the audience, rather than the presenter, comes up with the answer. If the audience reaches a conclusion acceptable to all, to use a common term in training circles, they will 'own' the solution. They will then be more committed to that solution than if they had it imposed on them by someone else.

The principal danger with this approach is that a discussion group can take on the characteristics of a rogue elephant in that they can be totally unpredictable. There is, therefore, no guarantee that the discussion group will necessarily cover the issues which you wanted them to examine. Hence, it can be important to have someone (probably the presenter) act as a 'facilitator' to direct the course of the discussion. How is this done? By judicious use of questions intended to make the group test the validity of the arguments they are putting forward and, hopefully, reconsider the direction the discussion is taking.

If all the members of the discussion group are to be able to participate effectively, each group should not be too large. Ideally the groups should be between four and six in number and certainly should not exceed 10. Again ideally, the presenter should act as a facilitator participating *throughout* the group discussion. Where the audience exceeds the ideal numbers for a single discussion group, they will have to be broken down into several groups each with their own facilitator. It is possible for the facilitator (or facilitators) to move from group to group but this will reduce their ability to control the discussions.

If the issues are being discussed simultaneously by two or more groups, you should build into the timetable time for the groups to report back collectively in a plenary session. If you decide to adopt this approach, you should tell the groups this will happen before they start discussing the issues. If you fail to do so, you may find particular groups have failed to keep a note of their discussions.

Is there any ideal length for a discussion group session? The session must be long enough for the issues to be examined but not so long as to give the group an opportunity to go round in circles on a few points. On that basis (and assuming the ideal size of group), whatever the topic the discussion session is unlikely to have value if it lasts less than 15 minutes. The laws of diminishing returns would certainly strike once the session lasted much more than 45 minutes.

The case-study approach

This is the ultimate illustration of the 'I do, I understand' tenet of the educational theory.

This approach involves presenting the audience with a factual situation and requiring them to exercise their knowledge or skills to reach a conclusion. A simple illustration would be where the objective of the presentation is to explain to junior lawyers how to approach a particular type of transaction.

Getting them to 'do' the transaction in the safe environment of the training room has a number of advantages over making them handle the transaction for the first time on behalf of a real client. First, it always takes longer to do anything when it is first encountered. Therefore, someone doing a transaction for the first time is likely to spend longer on it than if they have encountered the problems before. Many firms will take the inexperience of the lawyer handling the task into account when assessing the final bill. There is, nevertheless, the risk that the client will have to pay more in the circumstances because of the time taken by an experienced lawyer to check the work of the junior. Secondly, most transactions have unique features and having done a particular transaction for one client does not necessarily mean that there will not be further learning for the lawyer to do when he or she comes across a second similar transaction. If the case study approach is used for training, the person preparing the case study can ensure that it does cover the key issues which usually arise in transactions of the particular type. This approach will mean that a lawyer who has been on the training programme will understand the key points to be addressed in similar transactions for a variety of clients and will only have to get to grips with the unique features in each case. The trained lawyer, therefore, will have less learning to do on each transaction and is therefore likely to be more efficient and less prone to making errors.

Obviously, suggesting every lawyer should be trained by this method before dealing with any particular transaction is the ideal which may be unrealistic in practice. This does not negate the principles explained in the preceding paragraph. If the number of young lawyers who are about to start doing a particular transaction is insufficient to justify running a case-study-based training programme just for them, a mixed-ability group could be put together. This will have the advantage that the inexperienced young lawyers will learn from the practical experience of their seniors. The more experienced lawyers will be able to hone the techniques they have picked up on-the-job.

This book is not advocating that learning on the job is of little educational value; far from it, since dealing with a real-live problem for a real-live client can get the mind working faster, more creatively and more effectively than will necessarily be the case in a training situation. However, introducing junior lawyers to the concept of a transaction in a training room will get them one or two rungs up the ladder in terms of knowledge and speed their progression up the learning curve.

How are case studies developed? They should be based in reality so as to ensure that the lessons learned have maximum use in the office. Case studies can be relatively easily developed by taking the facts from real cases and adjusting them to cover the points which the training session is designed to address.

It is possible to construct a case study which can be worked on by an individual. For example, presenting him or her with a set of facts and requiring the individual, say, to draft or amend a document in accordance with the facts. However, it is often more beneficial to have teams working on the case study. If the case study is examining a transaction with two sides, one team can be instructed to act for, say, the purchaser, while the other acts for the vendor. Such a case study is likely to involve a discussion group as well.

How long should the case study last? There can be no hard-and-fast rule since it depends how detailed the case study is going to be. A case study on a legal drafting course could involve redrafting two or three lines from a clause and take five or 10 minutes. Alternatively, a comprehensive case study designed to hone the skills of young litigators could last days if they are expected to follow a case through all the stages from initial instructions to trial or settlement.

Writing a case study from scratch requires expert knowledge by the presenter and putting together a comprehensive case study can be very time consuming. The time can be shortened by using a real case. However, it would be dangerous to simply lift a real case from your files unchanged without careful consideration of whether the case was sufficiently typical to be of real educational value.

As with discussion groups, to be effective this approach needs a relatively low tutor–student ratio. The discussion above of numbers for an effective discussion group applies equally to an effective case-study group.

Role-plays

Role-playing is another participative method and can easily be combined with the case study. As the name implies, the members of the audience take on roles and act out the situation. Role-plays are of considerable value when teaching or honing interpersonal skills such as interviewing, negotiation or advocacy.

The guidelines on length given for discussion groups and case studies above apply equally to role-plays. So far as the staff–student ratio point is concerned, the ratio should ideally be much lower. For example, if the students are being trained on how to interview, the role-play will most likely involve one student playing the part of the interviewer and one playing the part of the interviewee. If the performance of the interviewer is to be properly reviewed, the interview needs to have been watched by the trainer (or at any rate someone with experience of interviewing). In reality, the staff–student ratio for role-plays will depend on the nature of the role-play. For example, it may be possible for the trainer to review the performance of a larger number of students who have undertaken a mock negotiation, but when it comes to advocacy the nature of the skill being tested means that individual feedback is required.

There has been a reference to 'feedback'. What does this entail? Any review of performance (or 'feedback') involves criticism but it is important that criticism should always be constructive, informative and include suggestions for improvements on which the presenter can act. The person giving the feedback should ensure that he or she comments on specific points, avoids generalities and should ensure that the suggestions help the student improve his or her performance, not destroy his or her confidence. The points for which the presenter will be looking in the student's performance will depend on the subject-matter of the training programme. For example, in an interviewing skills course, the presenter will be looking at whether the student extracted the correct information from the interviewee (among other matters); on an advocacy skills course, the presenter will be looking to see how the student marshalled the arguments in support of the imaginary client's case (again among other points). The task of giving feedback can be made much easier if the presenter has access to a video camera and can record the role-play. The tape can then be played back to the participant who will be able to see and hear his or her performance. Care needs to be taken with video-tapes. If the participant has never seen a recording of him or herself, the participant may concentrate on the wrong things. For example, the participant may be concerned about his or her voice and not notice what he or she is *saying*. The presenter should ensure this error does not occur.

Which method is best?

No one method is ideal in all possible circumstances. For a variety of purely practical or logistical reasons, the choice may be limited. Subject to that, the best approach is to mix and match the techniques to suit the circumstances. Returning to the illustration of the course for litigators, while the whole programme may be based on a case study, all the other methods could effectively be included. A *brief* talking-head session will be needed to introduce the whole training programme and to explain the structure of the case study. There may be technical topics to be covered in the training programme (such as an examination of the law of evidence or the rules on discovery) for which a talking head is the only sensible approach. Role-plays could be introduced so that the young lawyers on the programme could practise their interviewing techniques (when receiving initial instructions from the client) and their advocacy skills (for example, when the case study requires them to make an application before the master or registrar). The young lawyers could be broken up into discussion groups to agree on the advice they will give to the client following the initial meeting. The course leaders could use the questioning approach to test the young lawyers' knowledge of the relevant rules and procedure from the White or Green Books.

3.5   THE CONCLUSION

3.5.1   How long should the conclusion be?

The conclusion should probably represent no less than 5 per cent and no more than 15 per cent of the whole presentation; in any event it must not last longer than 10 minutes and should probably be shorter.

3.5.2   What should the conclusion contain?

This is the third stage of the 'Golden Three' and therefore it should *repeat* whatever you have identified as being the key messages or items of information you are trying to get across to the audience. You should draw the threads of your presentation together but not introduce new material. Suppose the presentation is at a client meeting at which you are giving your recommendation on how the client should proceed on a particular matter. In the main body of your talk you will have considered the client's position, the legal and other relevant problems this poses and the possible solutions. In the conclusion you should give your recommendation on which of the possible solutions the client should adopt.

It is important that the client in this illustration and your audience at more formal presentations are left in no doubt about the message you are endeavouring to get across. It could be a course of action which will help the client out of a difficult position, it could be guidance on the key aspects of a difficult area of law or it could be proof that your firm has advantages over rival firms seeking work. While the nature of the subject-matter may militate against this, ideally every presentation will end on an upbeat note.

3.6   IMPORTANCE OF REHEARSAL

Once you have completed the initial preparation and structuring stages, you now move into the rehearsal stage.

An orchestra will rehearse a piece exhaustively to ensure their delivery is perfect at the performance. Similarly, no actor would dream of going on stage without going through perhaps weeks of rehearsals. A presenter should adopt the same general approach.

Your preparation schedule (whether you have three hours or three weeks to prepare) should include time for you to rehearse your presentation. The more opportunities you have to rehearse, the greater will be the degree of your familiarity with the presentation and the greater will be the chances that the presentation will be a success.

You should allow yourself, come what may, at least one opportunity to give your presentation in 'real time'. What is meant by rehearsing in 'real time'? There is a temptation (to which most presenters succumb) to rehearse by merely reading their speech through to themselves (assuming a talking-head approach has been adopted). The danger with this type of rehearsal is that merely reading the text (as opposed to reading it out loud) will mislead you about how long the presentation will take. Once on your feet and with the audience staring at you, the tendency is to speak slower than normal. If you do not read the text out loud, you will find that in real life the presentation takes probably 10–20 per cent longer to deliver than you had expected.

It may seem somewhat eccentric to read the text aloud to yourself. However, doing so will give you a more accurate assessment of the likely length of time the presentation will take. Furthermore, your own self-critical faculties will come into play and help you decide whether you are, indeed, getting your messages across effectively. It is even more beneficial to present the information to colleagues. Not only will they be able to give advice on the technical content of the presentation but they will also be able to give a view on how well you are putting across the information.

If you are using any or all of the other training methods described in 3.4.3, it may be difficult to rehearse, for example, a discussion group. You will, nevertheless, need to be clear in your own mind how you intend to run it. How will you explain the way the discussion group will function? How do you intend ensuring the group covers the points you wish them to address? Do you intend the groups to report back in plenary session?

Rehearsal is vital when you are using any presentation aids. If you are using visual aids, do you know which visual aid to use at which moment in your presentation? How do you intend using the visual aids? If there are documents to be used in the course of the presentation, do you know your way around them? A brilliant presentation can be completely destroyed by poor use of these presentational aids. Guidance on how best to use them is given in chapter 6.

Save in the case of presentations which have to be delivered at extremely short notice, your preparation schedule should include time for adjusting your presentation after the initial rehearsal. After any necessary adjustments have been made, there should ideally be time for a further full dress rehearsal. At the further rehearsal, the complete presentation in its final form, including full use of presentation aids, should be delivered, if possible, in the location where the presentation will be given.

To repeat the warning to lecturers given at the beginning of this chapter: 'Fail to prepare, prepare to fail'. Rehearsal is an essential element of preparing to give a presentation. Failing to rehearse will negate much of the hard work you have put into preparing.

3.7 SUMMARY

(a)   Identify in your mind the objectives of the presentation.

(b)   Structure the information you have gathered using the 'Golden Three' approach in the order logic requires to achieve your objectives.

(c)   Decide on the most appropriate method for getting your message across.

(d)   Rehearse, rehearse and rehearse again.

Chapter Four

The Third Step to Effective Communication: Effective Delivery of the Presentation

4.1 INTRODUCTION

The final stage of any presentation is its delivery. This is the point at which you will, in effect, put out for inspection by the audience all the effort you have put into the initial preparation and structuring stages. For many people this can be a deeply traumatic experience. For some people the prospect of standing up in front of the audience, especially if it is large, is terrifying. For many, if not most, people there is the fear that the audience will reject what they have to offer. This may be in terms of the content of their talk: 'It was at too basic a level for me'; 'She did not know about the recent case'; 'I thought he was going to be talking about something completely different'. Even worse is the prospect of the audience rejecting the speaker personally: 'He was *so* boring'; 'She was completely incomprehensible'; 'How could anyone as nervous as that be given that degree of responsibility?'

If faced with adverse reaction to the content of the presentation, the speaker has failed to complete the initial preparation and structuring stages properly. If faced with an adverse reaction to him or her personally, the speaker has not addressed the third key element of preparing for a presentation, namely ensuring that the material is effectively delivered. In this chapter, guidelines are given on how to deliver your message or information in the most effective way whatever the situation. The chapter will, therefore, consider:

(a)   The presenter's delivery motto.

(b)   Guidelines on effective methods of oral communication.

(c)   The physical aspects of a presentation (covering the use of voice, eye contact, hands, stance and dress).

4.2   THE PRESENTER'S DELIVERY MOTTO

Once you know what you are going to say, and the order in which you are going to say it, you have to decide *how* you are going to say it. The way you say it must be determined by who you are. Therefore, it is useful to bear the presenter's delivery motto in mind:

Be yourself, be calm, be enthusiastic.

4.2.1   Be yourself

Many inexperienced presenters study the techniques used by good speakers they know. This is an excellent way of picking up points but should not be taken too far. If, for example, you are by nature an extrovert, you should not suppress your personality because you have been impressed by a speaker with a calm, low-key style of delivery. If you attempt this, you will probably put more effort into dampening your normally high spirits than into ensuring you get your message across. The audience may, therefore, be left with the impression of you as a very dull individual.

Whatever the nature of their personalities, very few people experience any significant difficulty in communicating on a purely social level. On the basis that a presentation is interpersonal human communication, there is no reason why you should not adopt your social communication style when presenting to *any* audience. This should be easy advice to put into practice when you are presenting on a one-to-one basis. However, nerves or a mistaken belief that a formal presentation to a large audience requires a more formal style, may prevent this happening in other situations.

4.2.2 Be calm

Many a presentation has been ruined by nerves reducing the speaker to a sweating, quivering, gibbering wreck. There are very few presenters, irrespective of their level of experience, who do not experience nerves to some extent before or during a presentation. For the majority of experienced speakers, experience merely reduces their level of nervousness (or has helped them learn techniques for controlling nerves) rather than removing it altogether. Some degree of nervous tension can be, in fact, very useful as it gets the adrenalin going which will help you focus on delivering effectively. Problems will only arise if the degree of nervousness from which you suffer is sufficient to cripple you as an effective presenter.

The principal cause of nerves is the feeling that something about the presentation will go wrong. Proper preparation should avoid this so far as content and structure are concerned. Adequate rehearsal will prevent this so far as delivery (including the use of visual aids) is concerned. If the cause of nerves is simply the prospect of making the presentation, relaxation techniques can be used.

It is not the purpose of this book to give detailed guidance on methods of relaxation since there are many books available on the subject. However, put simply, nerves can cause muscle tension and over-rapid breathing. If your muscles are tense, you will be unable to feel comfortable and your mind will not be able to concentrate on your delivery. The secret is to find ways of relaxing the muscles (flexing and unflexing the muscles should do the job). However, great care should be taken with this and expert advice should be sought if necessary.

Breathing too rapidly will inevitably interrupt the flow of your sentences. The audience will notice it if you break sentences at inappropriate points which will in turn increase your nerves. A simple method for controlling nerves generally is to breath deeply but calmly. However, care should be taken not to overdo this as it can lead to hyperventilation.

4.2.3   Be enthusiastic

If you are interested in your topic you should be able to generate interest in it among the audience, provided you guard against the risk of getting carried away by your theme. If you are bored by your subject, you will communicate that feeling to the audience.

Therefore, if you are trying to ensure your audience take in your message or your information, make the audience want to listen to you by generating enthusiasm for the topic. Enthusiasm must be genuine; the audience will see through you if you use inappropriate words (for example, by describing an incontrovertibly dull subject as 'fascinating'). They also need to *see* that you are enthusiastic as well as *hear* that you are. So long as genuine enthusiasm is present in you, you will be able to carry the audience along.

4.3   EFFECTIVE DELIVERY OF YOUR MESSAGE

It has already been said in this book that most people's level of comprehension is such that they can understand 400–600 words per minute whereas most people speak at a rate of only 150–200 words per minute (and in a presentation this rate could be lower). Your audience, therefore, has plenty of spare comprehension capacity and, unless you are careful, individual members of the audience will let their minds wander while you are talking.

Furthermore, while language is one of the vehicles of communication, it is by no means the only one. The way a sentence is constructed obviously has an impact on the message the speaker gets across. However, so does the inflection put on the words and the gestures used to go with them. Indeed, very clear messages can be sent and received without any words being spoken at all. Research has been done to find out what 'vehicles of communication' audiences use to decide whether they believe in the speaker's message. The purpose of the test was to assess which of the three main possible vehicles of communication (speech, inflection and expression/gesture) carried the most weight. Perhaps surprisingly, the words used were the least important by a long way, with inflection trailing expression/gesture.

Everyone has slept through presentations given by a knowledgeable speaker who delivered his or her talk in a dull monotone. Equally, everyone has been convinced by relatively lightweight presentations given by engaging speakers. The ideal is to mix the good character traits of these two types of speaker. Doing so will avoid the presenter's nightmare, a 'silent scream' (in other words, a yawn). The physical aspects of presentations will be examined in 4.4. This section will concentrate on giving guidance on delivery techniques which apply irrespective of the circumstances in which the presentation is being delivered.

4.3.1 Help, do not hinder, the audience's understanding

Even if your audience is familiar with the topic, they will not have heard your particular presentation before. Once you have presented an item of information, the audience will either understand it or not. If they do not understand the point you have just made, there will be a gap in their understanding. How much of a problem that gap will cause will depend on the importance to the rest of your presentation of the point the audience missed. Unlike when reading a book or playing a video, the audience cannot reread a section they did not understand or rewind a section they did not hear.

While it may be self-evidently good advice to help the audience understand your message, how is this done? To find the answer, you should consider the reasons why audiences do not understand the points made by speakers. There are many possible explanations. The first and most obvious is that the item of information was presented by the speaker in a way which was not comprehensible to the audience. This can be because the speaker has misunderstood the nature of the audience and makes excessive use of technical jargon or simply pitches the talk at too high a level. The speaker may have attempted to cover too much and has overwhelmed the audience with detail. All these are errors made in the preparation stages.

Even if the presenter has prepared properly for the presentation, he or she can still lose the audience if they do not understand at any given moment where they have reached within the presentation. This problem can be avoided by 'paragraphing' the points. By way of a simple illustration, if the speaker has decided there are five key points which need to be covered, he or she should highlight the *number* of points to be covered in the introduction. Having done so, the audience can be given clear guidance on where they have reached in the presenter's progression through his or her theme by being told which of the five points are being covered at any given time. Putting it simply, the presenter could deliver the main body of his talk along the following lines:

> In my introduction, I said there were five key points you will need to understand. The first of these is . . .. Having dealt with the first point, I now move to the second . . ..

And so on.

This technique of numbering points may not be appropriate to every circumstance and can be irritating to the audience. The same effect of signalling to the audience that one point has been completed and a new one is being introduced can be achieved by a form of words along the lines of:

> Having dealt with the issue of . . ., I imagine the question which has sprung into the minds of many of you is . . ..'

This technique should leave the audience in no doubt that a new point is being introduced. By using the device of asking a question which you then answer, you can impress the audience if the question posed has indeed sprung into their minds.

4.3.2   Speak to the audience, do not read to the audience

All presentations (including those over the telephone) involve interpersonal communication between the speaker and the audience. Although the degree of formality which applies to presentations can vary, in *every* case you should try to speak to the audience (irrespective of the size of the audience) as if you were having a social conversation with them. This approach will help you develop a rapport with the audience which will in turn help establish your credibility and therefore their confidence in you.

If that is the case, why do many presenters, especially when giving formal lectures, present their message or information by, in effect, reading a letter out to the audience? This theme is developed more fully in chapter 5. However, briefly, the reason is that many speakers preparing to give a formal presentation on a complex topic understandably feel the need for a complete script of their talk. The tendency is to reach for the dictating machine or pen and set out the information in the same way as they would when writing a client a letter. This often means that the script is written in the passive, rather than the active voice and the word forms are too legalistic. The problem can be compounded if the speaker places total reliance on the script and reads it out word for word. The audience will probably feel that they can read the letter the speaker has apparently written to them quicker than he or she can read it out and so save everyone a lot of time.

The way to avoid this is to ensure that any script you prepare is converted into a document which is written in a conversational style. Therefore, it should be written in the first or second person, with heavy use made of the active rather than the passive voice. The sentences should be short and simple. You should insert pauses into the presentation. To you, any pause can seem to last an eternity. To the audience it will only last for a second or two and they will hardly notice it. Pauses are natural in conversation and in a presentation are beneficial since they give you a chance to collect your thoughts on the next point as well as giving the audience a chance to absorb the points just made.

In normal conversation, you would repeat a point if you were trying to emphasise it and would reword a point if you thought the person you were speaking to had not understood you. There is no reason why these techniques should not be used in a presentation. Similarly, in ordinary conversation, if you are trying to explain something you would illustrate it in some way. Therefore, in a presentation, using an anecdote from your personal experience is an extremely effective way of enlivening your presentation as well as aiding the audience's comprehension.

The ultimate aim is to make the audience believe that you are speaking off the cuff. The techniques in this section will help achieve this aim but having a full script which you slavishly follow (even if it is written in a conversational style) will always tempt you to read it out loud. The only way that the impression of speaking off the cuff can be achieved is by reducing your full script to a set of headline notes which act as an aide-mémoire rather than a detailed script. The techniques for developing these notes from a full script are explained in chapter 5.

A particularly effective device to use is to *memorise* the first and last few minutes of the presentation. This approach will enable you to construct carefully the opening and closing sections of your presentation and be sure that, in the heat of the moment, you do not stumble over your words or forget your key messages. You should, however, make sure you avoid looking like a schoolchild who is reciting a poem learnt by heart but not understood.

4.3.3   Inform the audience and enthuse them

The whole purpose of any presentation is to get messages or information across to the audience. If you have prepared well, you will achieve this aim. However, it can be equally important to generate enthusiasm among your audience to ensure they do something, whether it is to instruct you (following a beauty parade) or follow your advice (after a meeting with a client). A vexed question for a legal speaker is the extent to which you should enthuse them by using verbal tricks.

In an excellent book entitled *Our Masters' Voices* (published by Routledge), Max Atkinson has described the results of his researches into the way politicians construct their speeches. He describes in some detail the tricks they employ to sway audiences and to induce them to applaud.

Max Atkinson came to the attention of the public when he appeared in a Granada Television documentary which followed the training he gave to a novice public speaker who was to speak at the Social Democratic Party's 1984 Conference. She achieved the only standing ovation of any of the non-platform speakers.

In brief (and with apologies for oversimplification), the three main devices which Max Atkinson identified as being in common use by politicians were:

(a) *The 'Claptrap'*. This means what it says, namely, 'A trick, device, or language designed to catch applause' (according to the *Shorter Oxford English Dictionary*). To use Max Atkinson's own explanation, this trick involves structuring the way you deliver your message to make it as clear to the audience when they should applaud or cheer as if you had said 'Hip, hip, hooray' to them. Max Atkinson uses the analogy of 'Ready, steady, go' to explain how the audience is given notice that praise or an insult is on its way which they should applaud or cheer. The audience is usually 'readied' by a general introduction, 'steadied' by some remarks about the 'target' and then let 'go' by naming the individual.

(b) *Lists of three*. These have an air of unity or completeness and this trick has been illustrated throughout this book. For example, in 2.1 the *three* key elements of effective communication were identified as 'effective initial preparation, effective structuring and effective delivery'. Max Atkinson refers to research carried out into conversational communication which has shown that people unconsciously wait for the third element when the speaker embarks on a list. The audience is, therefore, more likely to remember and respond positively to lists with three elements to them and feel short-changed if the list has only two items in it.

(c) *Contrastive pairs*. As a way of engaging the audience's attention, speakers often present them with a puzzle, thus arousing their collective curiosity. The speaker will then answer it by, for example, contrasting the approach of one political party with that of another.

Max Atkinson goes on to examine other devices which politicians can use to increase the impact of their messages such as charisma, quotability and 'televisuality'. The nature of the presentations which most of the readers of this book are likely to make are such that these topics are of relatively limited relevance.

While these tricks can be impressive, is it really appropriate to use such verbal pyrotechnics in the presentations which lawyers are commonly called upon to make? They may have their place in beauty parade presentations. However, they almost certainly do not have any real value in the presentations lawyers normally find themselves giving over the telephone, at meetings or in lectures. There is a risk that the effort you put into thinking of impressive verbal constructions will take away too much of the time you should devote to preparing an informative talk. Nevertheless, the ideas which Max Atkinson has put forward are fascinating and can add sparkle to your delivery.

4.4   THE PHYSICAL ASPECTS OF A PRESENTATION

4.4.1   The voice

The voice is the principal method of conveying *hard* information albeit that non-verbal forms of communication may influence the extent to which the audience believes what is said. Therefore, it is important that you make the best use of this particular weapon in your armoury.

If you are likely to be making presentations regularly, particularly to large audiences, it is worthwhile taking especial care of your voice. If you lose it temporarily or damage it permanently, no amount of expressive non-verbal gestures will help you get across the detail of complex legal issues. Should you be faced with this level of use of your voice, you are strongly advised to look at the many books available on the market giving advice on voice care and development.

On the assumption that the readers of this book are more likely to be occasional speakers, there are a number of straightforward guidelines to bear in mind when making presentations.

The most important guideline is to ensure that you are audible. In a small meeting room or over the telephone this should be no problem, provided there is no external interference. At a presentation to a larger audience, you should ensure you are audible by projecting your voice, rather than shouting. The latter approach may achieve the desired result of being audible but will certainly strain your voice. How do you project your voice? By using your diaphragm to push air over your vocal cords with sufficient power for you to be audible at a distance without whatever you are saying coming out as a scream. An alternative way of looking at the same thing is to think in terms of making sure you project your voice to the front of your mouth. If in doubt, practise by comparing a shouted phrase with the same phrase spoken at a reasonable volume from the front of your mouth. The result produced by the latter approach will be more comfortable for both you and the audience.

Projecting your voice may make the sound audible but will not of itself make the words understandable. Therefore, you should use your tongue, teeth and lips to enunciate each word clearly and distinctly. If you bear this in mind, you will avoid mumbling and running words together, both of which are significant bars to understanding in any presentation, even if it is one-to-one on the telephone or in a small room.

You should avoid any tendency to drop your voice at the end of each sentence. This tendency can be exacerbated if you look down at your notes as you are coming to the end of each sentence. As your eyes (and possibly head) drop, your voice drops too and if you are unlucky the audience will eventually drop off to sleep.

When people speak slowly they may mumble; the reverse of that problem is gabbling or speaking too fast. The latter problem arises for several reasons. You may be nervous, in which case you should take steps to calm yourself (for example, by taking a few quick deep breaths). You may realise you are running out of time and attempt to solve the problem by trying to cram more information into the limited time available. It is better to omit information and maintain an acceptable speed of delivery. If you do omit information which you intended to give to the audience, you must be careful to ensure this does not have an adverse effect on some later aspect of your presentation. Further guidance on this technique is given in chapter 6.

Even the most fascinating subject-matter can become boring if the modulation of the presenter's voice is uninteresting. In ordinary conversation, you will vary the tone of your voice, often unconsciously, to emphasise important words or to help the listener understand what you are saying. It is best not to become too obsessed with vocal modulation. It can lead a nervous speaker to modulate his or her voice at random, which could produce an extraordinary and unpleasant singsong effect. It is better to rely on Nature to give you guidance on vocal modulation and always remember to deliver the presentation as if it were part of a social conversation.

It is worthwhile being aware of your own verbal mannerisms. (It is not always easy to identify your own verbal mannerisms; you may need help from someone else.) When you come to the end of a sentence or a thought in normal conversation, do you insert meaningless sounds (such as 'er' or 'um') simply to fill the silence? While there are few people who are so relentlessly articulate as never to have to do this in social conversation, doing so when presenting a topic on which you are supposedly an expert can give the audience the wrong impression about you. It may appear that you are groping for the next thought (which is not necessarily a bad thing if you are trying to give the impression of speaking off the cuff). However, it can also give the impression of uncertainty or lack of knowledge (which certainly is a bad thing). If you find yourself inserting these meaningless sounds into pauses, think about why you do it. Is it because you are afraid of the silence? Pauses can be effective ways of helping the audience absorb information. You should certainly use them but make sure they do not last too long otherwise the audience may believe you have no idea what to say next.

An alternative to the meaningless noise is to use favourite phrases from your normal speech patterns. Almost everyone has some of these which constantly crop up in conversation. Most people are not very clearly aware of using such phrases but they can include phrases such as: 'First and foremost', 'At this moment in time', 'Be that as it may'.

These favourite phrases are often used at the beginning of sentences as a way of getting the speaker's vocal chords working without the speaker's brain being engaged. In normal conversation, they may not be very noticeable, not least because normal conversation involves two or more people constantly exchanging points. However, with presentations, the speaker is the only one saying anything, often for a comparatively long period of time. There is, therefore, greater opportunity for the speaker to use his or her favourite phrases and greater opportunity for the audience to notice them. When taken to extremes, heavy use of favourite phrases can distract the audience's attention from the subject-matter to such an extent as to negate the whole point of the presentation. It is not unknown for speakers to find that the audience has counted the number of times they have used certain phrases rather than concentrating on the information they are trying to get across.

4.4.2 Eye contact

The importance of maintaining eye contact with your audience as a way of creating a bond between you cannot be underestimated. If you do not look at your audience, they will lose confidence in you. If you do not look at them, they may draw the conclusion that you are uncertain of your subject-matter. This will call into doubt whether all the information you are delivering can be trusted to be correct.

How do you maintain eye contact with the audience? The numbers in the audience will determine the precise approach you adopt but the general principle is the same. Ideally, you should look at the *eyes* of your 'target' but for no longer than is usual in normal social conversation (that is to say, probably no more than five seconds). You should not lock eyes with a member of your audience and try to stare them down, merely make contact and then move on. If for whatever reason you find it difficult to look at the eyes of your target, focus on the bridge of his or her nose. You should never look at people by focusing on a point anywhere below chin level, irrespective of their gender.

While it is easy to make and maintain eye contact when talking one-to-one, how is it done with larger groups? With medium-sized groups (say 10 or fewer) you should try to make eye contact with *every* member of the group at irregular intervals during the presentation. It is obviously not advisable to look at each member of the audience in a fixed order with monotonous regularity; the audience will believe you are a programmed robot. The better approach is to continue doing what you would do naturally, namely, let your eyes unconsciously dwell on particular sections of the audience.

With large audiences, it is more difficult to make eye contact with individuals but you should still try to make eye contact with the audience as a whole. The approach most commonly adopted in these circumstances is to choose three points in the audience, one on the left of the audience, one in the centre and one on the right. Then at random you should look at the faces of the people sitting around those points. While there may be comparatively few of the audience with whom you make direct eye contact, the general impression you create among the audience as a whole will be positive.

It has already been explained that maintaining eye contact can maintain the audience's collective belief in you. However, can the speaker derive any benefit from looking at the audience? The answer to that is an emphatic yes. By looking at the audience, you will be able to see if they are confused, lost or bored.

If they are confused, is it because you have not explained a point well? If so, you should consider repeating it, possibly having reworded it more clearly. If they are lost, it may be because you have not been paragraphing your points properly and therefore restating the stage of your presentation which you have reached may solve the problem. If they are bored, this may be more difficult to deal with. Enlivening your presentation by using humour may solve the problem but it may be ill-advised to attempt this if you have not prepared for it. An alternative way of bringing the audience's concentration level back up may be to give them an anecdote from your personal experience (provided it is relevant to the point you are making).

If you look into the audience, you may find more positive proof of their reaction to the talk. If you are lucky, you will see a 'nodder'. This is somebody who is nodding his or her head vigorously in agreement with what you have said. The converse is a 'shaker' who may be shaking his or her head in violent disagreement. The former can boost your confidence tremendously, the latter can deflate it. Save for the most confident presenters, it is probably best to seek out the former and avoid the latter.

4.4.3 Movement and gestures

To repeat advice which has already been given in this book, you should project your own personality at a presentation, not adopt an alternative which, for whatever reason, you believe to be appropriate. You should, however, avoid doing anything which is likely to antagonise or irritate the audience. Extravagant hand gestures can be a distraction for an audience trying to concentrate on your presentation; constant pacing by the presenter can have the same effect. A totally motionless speaker will be unexciting to watch, especially if the delivery is unemotional as well.

Clearly the better approach is to adopt some middle course. It can be effective to make a few hand gestures to underline key points. Some movement around the venue for the presentation can be beneficial as it indicates that the speaker is relaxed. However, care should be taken with this advice. It may be that such movement would not be appropriate, for example, at a meeting around a table with a client.

Concentrating on hands, it is worth remembering that many people find their hands shake when they are nervous. If that is the case for you, you should take care to conceal the fact. If the audience think you are nervous, they may doubt your credibility. Given this, what should you do with your hands?

If you are at a client meeting (and so almost certainly sitting down), it is easy to keep your hands out of sight under the table. Avoid the temptation to fiddle with any papers or pens on the desk; this will only have the effect of highlighting your nervousness.

If you are standing (which you are likely to be doing at a more formal presentation), you can conceal the shake in your hands by, for example, holding the lectern, if there is one. If there is no lectern, you can give your hands something to do, such as holding your notes. However, if your hands are shaking visibly, the shake will be magnified if you are holding a sheaf of white A4 pages.

An alternative would be to put your hands in your pockets (if you have any). This can give the impression of being relaxed and confident but not if, in your nervousness, you rattle any loose change in your pocket. An alternative approach which is both reasonably comfortable and unobtrusive is to clasp your hands behind your back in the way adopted by a number of members of the royal family. It is *not* advisable to cross your arms in front of your chest as this can both limit your attempts at projection and will look defensive. Crossing your hands in front of your body in what could be described as the 'fig-leaf' position also looks defensive and should be avoided.

So what is the best approach to adopt? The best advice is to try out the various suggestions in this section and find the one with which you are most comfortable.

4.4.4   Sit or stand?

Irrespective of the number of people in the audience and the layout of the room, it is always appropriate to stand when giving a presentation, unless the presentation is being given at a round-the-table meeting. Even in that case, it may be appropriate for the presenter to stand for part of the presentation, for example, when using visual aids.

The difficulty with sitting down to give a presentation is that it may inhibit your ability to project your voice because your diaphragm will be compressed. Furthermore, if you are sitting behind a table, the tendency will be to lean forward and rest on your elbows which will increase the compression of your diaphragm.

If the audience is sitting in rows and you sit in front of them, you will find it difficult, if not impossible, to make eye contact with the individuals sitting near the back of the room. Their view of you will be blocked by the heads of the people sitting in front of them. If the rows are long, you may also find it difficult to look naturally at the individuals at the ends of even the front row.

Conversely, if you stand correctly (with your weight evenly distributed on both feet and your back straight) your voice projection will not be inhibited. If you are standing and the audience is sitting, everyone should be able to see you. However, be careful to minimise the extent to which you shift your weight from foot to foot. Doing so to excess may highlight to the audience any nervousness you feel.

Standing up is certainly appropriate for a formal lecture but it may be too formal for the more participative training methods described in 3.4.3. In those situations, where you are trying to engender a more relaxed attitude, it may be sensible to compromise between standing and sitting by perching on the edge of a desk. It will certainly be important, if you have broken the audience up into groups to perform some task, to move around the groups to give guidance.

4.4.5 Dress

In very few cases will this cause problems for legal presenters since they will be making presentations in a work situation for which their normal work clothes will be appropriate. However, it can be embarrassing to be dressed inappropriately for the given situation. Therefore, if the dress code for the presentation is not obvious, you must check the point. You may feel at a disadvantage if, for example, you are asked to give some form of presentation at a weekend meeting with clients and arrive dressed casually only to find the clients in their normal business clothes.

4.5 SUMMARY

(a) Be yourself, be calm, be enthusiastic.

(b) Help your audience understand the presentation by giving them clear guidance through your topic.

(c) Treat the presentation as a social conversation using conversational word forms and therefore do not read your speech to them.

(d) Be careful to ensure the physical aspects of your presentation maximise the impact of your message and minimise the possibility of the audience being distracted.

Chapter Five

Presentation Aids: Visual Aids, Amplification and Documentation

5.1 WHAT ARE PRESENTATION AIDS?

A presentation aid is any aid which the speaker uses to help the audience understand or remember the presentation. As the chapter title explains, the nature and use of the following presentation aids will be considered:

(a) Visual aids.

(b) Amplification.

(c) Documentation.

These aids have been referred to elsewhere in the book (for example, documentation is dealt with briefly in 2.4.6 and visual aids are dealt with in 2.4.7). This chapter gives more detailed advice on the uses and advantages (as well as disadvantages) of these aids.

5.2 VISUAL AIDS

5.2.1 What is the purpose of a visual aid?

A visual aid should inform the audience, not confuse them; it should attract the audience's attention, not distract them; it should add to the presentation, not detract from it. The mere use of any visual aid will, momentarily at the very least, raise the concentration level of the audience. If it is designed and used well, the visual aid will help ensure the audience concentrate on the presentation and therefore remember it.

The preceding sentences give an indication in the broadest of terms of the advantages of using visual aids. Those sentences, however, give no guidance whatever on what visual aids you can use, how to design them or how to use them effectively. Guidance on each of these points is given in the succeeding paragraphs.

5.2.2   What visual aids are available?

Modern technology will give you access to a wide range of visual aids. In this section of the chapter, the advantages and disadvantages of the most commonly available visual aids are described together with an indication of the circumstances when it may be most appropriate to use each type of visual aid.

Flip charts, white and blackboards

What are they? A flip chart is a simple device which holds a sheaf of, usually, A3 pages on which you can write notes. Traditionally, flip charts stood alone but in many purpose-built conference centres and modern offices' meeting rooms the flip charts are hung from or attached to the wall. Whatever the nature of the flip chart, once you have finished with a sheet, you can tear it off the pad. This is the *only* way of removing one set of notes if the flip chart is attached in some way to the wall of the presentation venue. If it is free-standing, you can flip the sheet you have used over the back of the flip chart. This has the advantage that you are able to refer to that sheet again later in your presentation.

A whiteboard performs the same function as a blackboard (with which everyone is familiar). Whiteboards are produced in the colour of their name and are written on using pens rather than chalk.

When using any of these systems, you will normally have to produce the visual aid yourself by writing or drawing on the flip chart or board. It is possible to obtain professionally produced visual aids which fit on to a flip chart but these can be expensive. In the rest of this section, it is assumed that you will be writing or drawing the visual aid by hand.

These systems have the major advantage of being easy to produce (you can do it yourself) and are easy to use since there is virtually no technology which can go wrong. However, they are really only suitable for small audiences because they can be difficult to read in a big room, especially if your writing and/or drawing skills are not good. If the audience is very small, say a one-to-one meeting with a client, the same result can be achieved with a pen and a notepad. Although any visual aid can attract interest, it is difficult to make hand-made visuals look interesting. If you write or draw them in front of the audience, you will at least have the advantage of spontaneity. This approach is particularly helpful if you are noting the points which have come out of a discussion group (which obviously cannot be pre-prepared) or if you are building up a diagram of a transaction as a way of explaining it in easy stages to help the audience assimilate the information.

These systems can be very flexible since you will start with, in effect, a blank sheet and can produce almost anything (within the bounds of your personal abilities). Regrettably, if you wish to use the materials again, they are bulky to transport and can easily get torn or dirty.

Overhead projectors

Overhead projectors (OHPs) are devices for projecting, on to a screen, transparencies (usually A4 in size) or information written on a roll of transparent material attached to the machine.

Whether you are using transparencies or writing on the transparent roll, this form of visual aid is very easy to use. The images can be hand-written (in which case the problems of your handwriting and drawing skills will be relevant again) but it is also possible to print the transparencies. Computer software and hardware is available which can produce very sophisticated (and, in some cases, colourful) OHP slides. However, it is possible to print your own slides by using a PC to print out the text or (if possible) the drawing and then photocopying the hard copy on to an OHP transparency. To be most effective, you should use the largest print size on your printer. To increase the print size even further, produce the slide on A5 and then blow it up to A4 size by using a magnifying photocopier. This technique cannot be used when you are relying on the roll; any image on that has to be hand-written.

Overhead projectors are suitable for virtually any audience, but are probably over the top for small client meetings. The only limitation is whether the print size you have used coupled with the power of projection of the OHP is sufficient to ensure the slide is visible at the back of the room.

Although OHPs represent a higher level of technology than do flip charts, they are relatively simple devices and therefore easy to use. Unlike 35 mm slides, there is no complicated rule about which way to put the slide on to the machine. The nature of the projection is such that you can usually use an OHP without having to dim the lights in the room. There is, however, always the potential problem of the OHP bulb failing at the crucial moment.

The degree of interest which an OHP slide can generate will depend on the design. If the slide is hand-written, the contents may be the same as a flip-chart sheet but the fact that it is projected on to a screen will increase its impact. The system is very flexible in that you can use pre-prepared slides as well as creating them on the spot. Furthermore, you can use more sophisticated techniques such as reveals and overlays (which are described in more detail below). Furthermore, since the slides do not have to be kept in any particular order (as is the case with the flip chart or 35 mm slides) you have the added degree of flexibility of being able to keep going back to a particular slide without difficulty.

OHP slides are very durable, especially if they are put into clear plastic covers and are not too bulky to carry.

35mm slide projectors

Everyone is familiar with these. A slide projector can be used as a way of projecting notes or diagrams on to a screen but such slides are comparatively difficult and expensive to produce. The vast majority of lawyers who are thinking of using this type of visual aid will have to call upon the services of specialist companies offering slide design and production facilities. Once the slides are produced, they are more difficult to use than OHP slides. This is because they have to be carefully loaded into the projector cartridge (by being put in upside down and back to front). Although the projectors available on the market nowadays are generally highly efficient, there is always the risk of the projector jamming which can lead to the slides being damaged. As if a jammed projector is not enough of a problem, the projector may have to be physically separated from the speaker (for example, positioned at the back of the room) so as to project a large enough image. At best, this will increase the time it takes to solve the problem, at worst the speaker may have difficulty getting to the projector if the room is full. It is possible that the projector will not even be in the same room as the presentation, for example, if back projection facilities are available. However, venues which provide this type of sophisticated projection facility will almost certainly have a technician available who will be able to assist with solving any problems.

The major advantage of professionally produced 35 mm slides is that they look very impressive compared with OHP slides or flip charts. They are generally extremely good attention grabbers, especially if they are colourful and well designed. However, if the audience has been watching a series of presentations by speakers who use professionally produced 35 mm slides, any one slide's impact may not be much greater than any other type of visual aid. They are visible in almost any size room although the lights will need to be darkened if the slide is to have maximum effect. (This point is considered in more detail in chapter 6, but one problem with 35 mm slides is that their use may mean that while the slides can be seen, the audience will not have enough light to take notes.) A disadvantage of 35 mm slides is that they are not especially flexible. Once you have loaded the cartridge for the projector in a particular order, it is not easy to change that order. What if there is a particular slide the speaker wishes to use more than once in the course of his or her presentation? The speaker could simply return to the slide but this will involve backtracking through the cartridge. The audience will, therefore, see all the intervening slides, in reverse order, in a series of second-long flashes. This is at best an irritation to the average audience. Alternatively, the speaker can have a particular slide reproduced as many times as he or she will need to use it. This approach will avoid the problem of backtracking but will increase the number and therefore the cost of the slides.

This type of visual aid is probably most appropriate at formal, relatively large scale presentations at conferences.

35 mm slides can be easily damaged if they are in cardboard surrounds. Most, if not all, professionally produced 35mm slides have plastic surrounds which make the slides extremely hard-wearing. Being so small, they are easily portable.

Videos

As with 35 mm slides, these can be used in one of two ways. First, if the speaker wants the audience to participate in a role-play, he or she can record all the role-plays for subsequent playback using a video camera. Secondly, the speaker can use a prerecorded tape. Very few lawyers have access to video production facilities. Therefore, they are most likely to use professionally produced videos, which are difficult and expensive to produce. Although there are a large number of very good training videos on skills (such as negotiation or interviewing), there are comparatively few videos on technical legal topics (although this is beginning to change).

If the speaker can find a video which is suitable for the presentation, they are very easy to use except if the presenter wishes to rewind or fast-forward through the tape. In that case, the speaker must have played the video in advance to identify exactly where the points he or she wishes to show are located on the tape. This is done by using the counter facility which all video players have.

Videos can be used with any size audience, but will usually only be suitable as part of a presentation at a training seminar. If using a video is appropriate, the bigger the audience the more complicated the projection facilities must be. With large audiences, a number of television monitors or big-screen projection facilities may have to be used. For small audiences in small rooms using television monitors, natural lighting can be used. However, in bigger rooms and especially if the video is projected rather than played on a television monitor, the room will need to be darkened. Generally, the nature of the videos which lawyers are likely to use are such that the audience are unlikely to need to take notes. (In the coming years, there will be an increase in the use of videos in technical legal training with the advent of legal subscription television, which will have to be recorded for subsequent viewing, and monthly legal video updates. If that type of video is used in a darkened room, the problem of note-taking will become an issue.)

A video is a very effective way of maintaining the audience's concentration levels. Moving pictures are always more interesting than still ones. However, the limited number of suitable videos specifically targeted at the legal market means that the presenter runs the risk of the audience not perceiving the video as being relevant to their circumstances. This problem can be overcome by the careful introduction of the video.

The nature of videotape cassettes is such that they are hard to damage and easily portable.

5.2.3   How do you design and use visual aids?

Having read the previous section, you will know the range of visual-aids technology available. To summarise the key points, a flip chart (which for this purpose is intended to include white and blackboards) should only be used when you are dealing with a small audience, for example, at a client meeting or in a discussion group. Overhead projector slides (which for this purpose includes information written on the transparent roll on the projector) could be used in any presentation a lawyer is likely to give. 35 mm slides could be used in any presentation by a lawyer but their cost is such that they are likely to be used only at prestigious presentations, such as beauty parades or public conferences. Concentrating on professionally produced videos, the nature of the videos currently available is such that they are likely to be used principally as part of skills training programmes to reinforce the presenter's messages.

The nature of the presentation may, therefore, determine which visual aid technology you use. In any event, it is best not to mix technologies unless the circumstances really warrant it. For example, you could use an OHP to support a presentation prior to the delegates breaking up into discussion groups at which each group uses a flip chart to note the issues raised in the course of their discussions. Once you have decided on the technology you are going to use, you need to design the visual aid and use it effectively.

Designing visual aids

Ignoring videos, there are a number of simple guidelines to bear in mind when preparing *any* visual aid (whether you are using a flip chart, an OHP or a 35 mm projector). They are as follows:

(a)   Use pictures, rather than words (if possible). A picture is the quintessential visual aid and therefore you should *always* use some form of visual aid if you wish the audience to see something which cannot easily be described in words. Taking this a stage further, it would be even better to bring the item pictured with you to the presentation. This may not, however, be feasible. Although pictures are preferable, this is not to say that visual aids should never have words on them. However, be careful not to confuse your audience with a mass of text (as to which see below).

(b)   Use bullet points, not full sentences. If you decide you want to use words on your visual aids, encapsulate the point you are making in a single word or short phrase. If you put complete sentences on the visual aid, inevitably the print will have to be small and the visual aid may not be easy to read. There are limited circumstances in which you should put full text on to a visual aid. This can include when you are explaining the interpretation of a statutory provision or a clause in a document and you need the audience to see the phrase you are explaining in context.

(c)   Keep them short. On the face of it, this may not seem to be a problem with a picture. However, if you are using a visual aid, for example, to explain a complex transaction, the audience may be confused if they see a visual aid with *all* the stages of the transaction on it. It may be better to build up the transaction by a series of visual aids. If you have text on your visual aid, you should limit the number of bullet points on each visual aid. As a rough rule of thumb, there should be no more than five or six lines of text on any visual aid.

(d)   Use colour rather than black and white, if possible. All the main types of visual aid can be produced in colour. Pens for writing on flip-chart sheets and OHP slides are available in all the colours of the rainbow and a professionally produced 35 mm slide can and should be in colour. It is possible to obtain professionally produced colour OHP slides. However, if you are producing a printed OHP slide using your own PC, printer and photocopier, the slide you produce will be in black and white. You could, of course, hand-colour it after it has been printed. Care should be taken with the choice of colours. Some combinations of colours (for example, blue and green) look the same to people who are colour-blind. Certain colours (for example, yellow) do not always project very clearly.

(e)   Use graphs not figures, if possible. The audience will find a graph or pie chart summarising complex figures more comprehensible than the figures themselves. However, if your presentation involves an examination of a set of accounts, you will have no choice but to reproduce the accounts.

(f)   Do not use too many visuals. Although there is no optimum, minimum or maximum number of visual aids, you should not use too many in your talk. If you do, you will spend most of your time dealing with the visual aids rather than concentrating on your presentation.

(g)   Pre-prepare the visual aids, rather than create them on the spot (save for certain circumstances). If you adopt the approach of pre-preparing the slides, you will be able to use printed slides for the OHP and 35 mm projector (whether produced in-house or not) which will be legible (provided the slides are not too full). If you hand-write the slides, doing so beforehand will mean you can construct the flip-chart sheet or slide carefully. You can ensure the visual has a neat layout and contains all the information you want in a legible form. If you try to hand-write the visual at the presentation, first to minimise the waste of time, you will write quickly and therefore maximise the chances of the visual being difficult to read. Secondly, when you are writing, you cannot look at the audience and, especially if the visual is long or complex, it may take you some time to re-establish the bond with the audience. Thirdly, if you produce the visual aid in the session, there is always the chance that you will make a mistake which will adversely affect the impact of the visual aid and could confuse the audience. Nevertheless, producing the visual at the session has the benefit of spontaneity and may be necessary if you are, for example, using the visual aid to list points raised by the audience in the course of the presentation or in the course of a discussion. If you are using a visual aid to build up a picture of, for example, the structure of a transaction, it is a good idea to pre-prepare even this by lightly outlining in pencil the structure you will over-draw at the presentation. Obviously, this technique is of principal relevance when you are using a flip chart.

The use of visual aids

The most important guideline to bear in mind is that the visual aid (whatever it may be) must be relevant to the presentation and help the audience understand what you are saying. Pictures or graphs will help the audience visualise something which may be difficult to describe in words. Full text visuals should be avoided or at least kept to a minimum. However, visuals using bullet points (which should be kept short, simple and forceful) can help the audience understand the structure of your presentation and the point you have reached at any given time. They can help emphasise the main points. The guidelines for using any visual aid (other than a videotape) are as follows:

(a)   Incorporate the visual aid into your presentation. You should not leave the audience in any doubt about the relevance of the visual aid to the points you are making.

(b)   Display the visual aid when you need it, remove it when you do not. With an OHP slide this means turning on the OHP having already positioned the slide on the projector. With a 35 mm projector, project the slide. With a flip chart, show the relevant sheet. Merely displaying the visual aid will attract the audience's attention. The problems arise when you have finished with the visual aid. For an overhead projector slide, you should turn the OHP off first and *then* remove the slide. This prevents the audience being dazzled by the bright light projected by the OHP on to the screen. If you are using

35 mm slides, you can go on to the next slide but what if you do not want to use the next slide for some minutes? You can either turn the projector off or put blank slides into the projector's cartridge (again to avoid dazzling the audience). You can 'turn off' a flip chart by inserting blank sheets between each pre-prepared sheet. When you have finished with one sheet you can flip the sheet over and a blank sheet (which is of no interest to the audience) will be displayed.

(c)   Do not block sight-lines, and maintain eye contact with the audience. There is nothing worse than for you to spend time preparing visual aids only to destroy their impact by standing in a way which will prevent some of your audience seeing the visual aid. This problem can be avoided very easily by being aware of where the audience is sitting in relation to the visual aid you are displaying. The problem of blocking sight-lines most commonly arises when speakers use the overhead projector. There is a tendency when explaining some aspect of a slide to point at the slide on the projector itself. Depending on the position of the projector in relation to the audience, doing so will probably mean that the speaker is standing between the screen and some section of the audience. Although the layout of the particular venue may create difficulties, generally the simple solution is to use a pointer to indicate *on the screen* the aspect of the slide with which you are concerned. For reasons which have already been explained in this book, it is important that you maintain eye contact with the audience at all times. Therefore, do not turn your back on the audience and talk to the screen or flip chart. If nothing else, some of the audience may find it difficult to hear what you are saying.

(d)   Give the audience time to absorb the visual aid. There is no point producing a visual aid which you do not display for long enough to give the audience a chance to understand it. Equally, do not make it difficult for your audience to take on board the points you are making in relation to the visual aid itself. There is a natural tendency among audiences to take notes. This tendency will extend to copying any visual aids you have produced. Therefore, if your visual aids are reproduced in any materials the audience has or will receive, you should tell them.

(e)   Use the techniques of reveals and overlays to avoid giving all the information at once. Even if you follow the guidelines in this section, each visual aid may still contain a lot of information. If you display all this information at once, the audience may read all the points on the visual aid when they first see it. This will mean that they will not be able to concentrate on what you are saying. You can avoid this problem by using the technique of revealing. If you are using a pre-prepared OHP slide this merely entails covering the slide with a sheet of paper when you first project it and revealing the information on the slide point by point as you reach it in your presentation. You can achieve the same effect with a flip chart and 35 mm slides but this will entail producing a series of sheets or slides each with one additional point on it. This will be time-consuming and (in the case of 35 mm slides) expensive to produce. 'Overlaying' is the technique of building up a picture by adding a series of additional segments. The effect is easy to produce when using an OHP since you merely need to produce a series of slides each with, for example, a different aspect of the transaction you are explaining on them. Care obviously has to be taken to use the slides in the correct order to build up the full picture and to position them correctly. The same effect can be achieved using 35 mm slides but this will involve a series of separate slides with the resultant cost implications. Overlays are not possible with flip charts; the same effect can be achieved by drawing the transaction as you explain it in your presentation.

(f)   Guard against all eventualities. The obvious danger with any visual aid is that the technology may fail you. At first sight, you may think there is little which can go wrong with a flip-chart but what if you discover the flip chart has no sheaf of pages attached to it? What if the flip-chart pens do not work? Turning to OHPs, you may feel that the advice in this book of turning the projector on and off when you use each slide is potentially dangerous as it may blow the bulb. These projectors are very robust and most have a 'dual-bulb' facility (which means that if one bulb goes then, at the turn of a switch, a spare bulb, already fitted, will come into use). Even so, it is not a bad idea to carry a spare OHP bulb with you. In addition to the risk of jamming, 35 mm projectors can also suffer from bulb failure. To guard against this eventuality, especially if it is crucial to the audience's understanding that they see your visual aids, you should always ensure that copies of your slides (whether they are OHP or 35 mm) are distributed to the audience. Apart from anything else, this will save them from having to copy the information on the slides and they will have something on which they can write notes from your presentation.

(g)   Rehearse using the visual aids. If you are going to use visual aids, you must be able to incorporate them properly into your presentation. This will mean knowing exactly when to use which visual aid. The only way you can be sure that you will be able to use the visual aids smoothly is by rehearsing their use.

It is worth bearing in mind that the mere use of visual aids will not turn a bad presentation into a good one. They might, however, make a good presentation memorable.

5.3 AMPLIFICATION

If the venue for your presentation is large or the acoustics are bad, you should use some form of amplification system.

Most amplification systems come with two types of microphone, the neck microphone or the stand (or static) microphone. If you have a choice, a neck microphone is preferable because it will move around with you. You will, therefore, be free from the worry of moving out of the range of the microphone. The main problem you face with a neck microphone is the trailing wire from it to the amplifier. You should avoid tripping over this.

The problem with a static microphone is that although you may move, it will not. Therefore, you can move too close and deafen the audience or move away and become inaudible. While at first sight this may not seem to be a problem if you have rehearsed properly, what if you intend using OHP slides and the projector is some distance from the microphone? In that circumstance, you will either have to accept the pause in your presentation while you put on and take off each slide or arrange for someone to help you change the slides.

Since many people are not familiar with using microphones, you should always rehearse with the microphone. If you do not, you may find the experience of hearing your own voice amplified back to you disconcerting.

There is a tendency when using a microphone to remove some of the modulation from your voice out of a fear of deafening the audience. While care should be taken with the volume at which you pitch your voice, an amplified dull monotone is probably worse than one without the benefit of amplification.

5.4   DOCUMENTATION

5.4.1   What documentation needs to be prepared and why?

In the course of the initial preparation stage you should decide on whether your presentation will be helped by supporting documentation. In 2.4.6 it was recommended that you consider this issue from two angles, namely:

(a)   What documents, if any, you need to prepare for your own benefit.

(b)   What documents, if any, you need to prepare for the benefit of your audience.

The documents you prepare for your own benefit should be designed so that you will give the audience the impression that you are speaking off the cuff. They should, therefore, contain enough information to ensure you will be able to follow your carefully planned sequence of points. The documentation you prepare for the audience should contain whatever information you wish them to take away from the presentation and, if appropriate, should give them guidance through your presentation as you deliver it. The following paragraphs develop these ideas.

5.4.2   The documents you prepare for your own benefit

The documents you will prepare for your own benefit will be your notes. As with so much of the advice contained in this book, it will be the circumstances of the presentation which will determine the format of your notes. Taking it as read that you will prepare notes of some description to help you deliver the presentation, what form will they take? Your natural inclination will probably be to produce either a set of brief, bullet-point notes which will merely act as memory joggers or something much fuller, even a verbatim script. If it is one of your aims to give your audience the impression that you are speaking off the cuff, the former approach (of using brief bullet-point notes) will help you achieve your aim while the latter approach (of using a verbatim script) will hinder your aim.

When you are going through the structuring stage of preparation, one of the steps is to write the text of your presentation. The likelihood is that if you are planning to make a presentation on a subject with which you are familiar at a one-to-one client meeting, you will merely produce the bullet-point style of notes. You may even feel sufficiently confident with your knowledge of the subject that you will rely on your knowledge of the subject and past experience of this form of presentation. The converse will be the case if you are preparing to give an hour-long lecture on a highly complex area of law to a large audience of experts in the field. In those circumstances, you will probably wish to put together a detailed set of notes which will, in effect, amount to a verbatim script. Relying on a verbatim script will certainly give you the security of knowing you will cover all the key points. However, there is a real risk that you will fall into the trap of relying so heavily on the script that you read it out. The audience is unlikely to be impressed by the image of a speaker who appears to be so uncertain of his or her topic that he or she has to read out a pre-prepared text. At best, your audience may feel you are reading a letter to them which they could read to themselves far more quickly. At worst, they may begin to suspect that someone else has written your speech for you.

If the circumstances justify starting with a verbatim script, how do you convert them into briefer notes which will give the audience the impression you are speaking off the cuff? The first step is to hone your verbatim script to the point where you are totally satisfied with both the content and the phraseology. To reach this stage, you will probably have to rehearse the presentation more than once. Once satisfied with the text, you can follow one of two courses. You could extract from your verbatim script the keywords and phrases, putting them on to a series of cards. You are likely to have spent a considerable amount of time preparing for an important presentation and will probably find that merely seeing the keywords or phrases will trigger the thoughts behind them. If you do not have the full text of your speech, it will be quite impossible for you to read to the audience. Therefore, inevitably, you will speak off the cuff. This approach has both disadvantages and advantages. The keywords or phrases may trigger the relevant thoughts but not your carefully honed phrasing. You may not, therefore, deliver the information in as elegant a way as you may wish. If you do speak off the cuff making the wording, if not the thoughts, up as you go along, you will find it more difficult to control the length of the presentation.

As an alternative to the bullet point notes approach, you could retain the verbatim script but design it in a way which will maximise your chances of giving the impression of speaking off the cuff even though you are in reality reading. You are likely to read your material if that is the only way you can be sure of extracting and delivering the information it contains, which is likely to be the case if your script is typed in the way that a letter is laid out. You could be faced with pages of single-spaced typing with few breaks. Many speakers experience nervous dyslexia to some degree when presenting and this layout will only add to the problem.

Therefore, a better approach is to lay out your script so that the lines are double or even treble-spaced. Each sentence should start on a new line and, ideally, each paragraph (and therefore each new thought or concept) should start on a new page. This approach may produce a script which is tens of pages long (albeit that each page can be read fairly quickly) and so you should be circumspect about this last aspect of the advice. Laying out your script in this way will help you keep a track of the points you are trying to make. You will be helped even further if, for example, the keywords and phrases in the verbatim script are capitalised and/or highlighted. Using a script designed in this way, you will be able to glance down and the next thought should spring out of the page at you.

On the basis that with any presentation it is advisable to plan for the worst, preparing a detailed script is very useful should you be unable to make the presentation due to illness or other commitments. Your detailed script can be given to a substitute who will at least know the points you intended to cover. Chapter 6 contains advice on this problem and so that advice is not repeated here.

5.4.3 The documents you prepare for the benefit of the audience

The circumstances may determine this issue. In the case of client meetings it will almost certainly be self-evident what is required. It is sensible to issue documentation beforehand if the meeting has been called to consider some document you have drafted. If the purpose of the meeting is to consider the options available to a client in a particular circumstance, you will probably think it appropriate to confirm the advice you have given in a letter sent to the client after the meeting. It may not, however, be so clear with more formal training sessions. The rest of this section concentrates on the latter situation.

External pressures imposed on you by the presentation organisers may determine what, if any, documents you produce to help your audience. If you have complete freedom, you could produce documents to be handed out before or after the presentation. When you have structured the presentation so as to maximise audience participation (for example, by using discussion groups or a case study) it is always advisable to give some if not all of the documents to the audience in advance so that they can get to grips with the subject-matter beforehand. The issue of what documents, if any, you produce for the audience's benefit is, therefore, principally of relevance to talking-head presentations.

The most helpful approach is to produce a brief lecture outline which you distribute to your audience at the beginning of a presentation. This can be backed up with a full set of notes covering the points you made in your presentation plus any other relevant material. From the audience's point of view, the outline notes will mean they can see at a glance the structure of the presentation you have chosen to follow. If any point you make strikes a particular chord with a member of the audience, he or she can then record it on the outline and will then have a permanent record both of the point you made and the context in which you made it. The outline will also help if members of your audience lose concentration momentarily. A glance at the outline will tell them where you have reached and they will, hopefully, be able to continue following your presentation. The outline can, therefore, be the written equivalent of paragraphing (see chapter 4).

How should the outline be constructed? If it is to be most helpful to the audience, it should contain brief summaries of each of the points you make in the order in which you intend to make them. These summaries could be merely bullet points or something fuller (such as a sentence or two summarising a statutory provision followed by the section number). The outline should not be so full as to amount to the text of the speech. If it is, the audience will be tempted to read it. Some presenters issue outlines with the notes printed up on one half of the page so that the audience can take notes on the other half. Other presenters have the outline covering the entire width of the sheet but leave the facing page blank for notes. Whichever approach you adopt, make sure the audience has enough space to write whatever notes they wish against your notes. It can be extremely confusing for a member of your audience to pick up your lecture outline some months after the event and then to have to work out to which of your printed notes a scribbled comment applies.

After the event you could issue the verbatim text of your presentation. However, it will probably be more useful to the audience if the materials you issue at the end are fuller than your presentation.

If you have followed the advice in 5.2.3, you will have prepared for the risk of any visual aids technology you are planning to use breaking down by having copies of your visual aids available for distribution. If the visual aids repeat the information contained in your outline, there is no point handing out the same information twice. If the outline and the visual aids contain different information, it is certainly advisable to issue copies at the *end* of the presentation. Issuing them earlier will reduce their impact although the circumstances may justify doing so.

Whatever approach you adopt to the production of documentation for your audience, you should make sure the audience are clear about how to use the documentation they have received from the outset.

If you are part of the panel of speakers at a public conference, the organiser will give you instructions on the documentation required from you. You should find out when in the presentation the documentation will be issued. If you are asked to provide the text of your presentation or a fuller paper, try to prevent it being issued *before* your presentation. If this material is issued to the audience, they are likely to follow your presentation. The result is that you may find at certain points what you are saying is drowned out by the sound of the entire audience turning the pages of your paper simultaneously. Some organisers insist on distributing this material before the presentations begin. If you find yourself in this position, you can avoid the problem of simultaneous page-turning by covering the same material but in a different order or by producing a detailed paper for the organiser to distribute from which you select key points to examine in detail.

5.5 SUMMARY

The purpose of any presentation aid is to help, not hinder, you in presenting your message or information effectively to the audience. They are, needless to say, not compulsory but may help make the presentation memorable in the minds of your audience.

The key points to bear in mind when using visual aids are:

(a)   Keep them short.

(b)   Use bullet points.

(c)   Use pictures and colours.

(d)   Incorporate the visual aid into your presentation.

(e)   Do not leave the visual aid on display longer than necessary.

(f)   Do not block the audience's sight-lines.

The key points to bear in mind in relation to documentation are that the documents you produce to help yourself should be designed so that you give the impression of presenting the material off the cuff even if that is not the reality of the situation. The documents you produce for the benefit of your audience should help them understand the presentation as it is being delivered and ensure that they remember the key messages afterwards.

Chapter Six

Potential Problems and How to Avoid Them

6.1 INTRODUCTION

In this chapter on the potential problems which can arise in relation to presentations, the warning to bear in mind is:

If it can go wrong, it will go wrong.

While that motto is particularly worth bearing in mind when dealing with the presentation technology described in chapter 5, it applies to a wide variety of aspects of any presentation. This chapter considers the most common problems which can arise:

(a) Before a presentation.

(b) During a presentation.

(c) After a presentation.

The problems examined are those you are most likely to encounter; the coverage cannot be comprehensive. The problems described in this chapter can all be easily overcome by being aware that they could arise and planning for them. As with life generally, some problems you may face at a presentation cannot be anticipated. If you are unfortunate enough to find yourself facing such a problem, you will have to find the solution on your own.

6.2   BEFORE THE PRESENTATION

While you are going through the preparation stages for the presentation, you should have in mind the logistics of the presentation to ensure that the presentation runs smoothly.

6.2.1   The programme for the presentation

You must be aware of the timetable into which your presentation will fit. At what time in the day will you be making your presentation? For reasons which were explained in chapter 3, the degree of receptiveness among your audience may differ depending on the time you are making your presentation to them.

If you are taking part in a presentation involving other speakers, where does your presentation fit into the overall programme? If there are other speakers involved in the presentation, you must liaise with them to make sure that your presentations complement each other and do not conflict. At the very least, you should find out the titles of the other speakers' presentations. If you think there is any risk of overlap, obtain an indication of what the other speakers will be covering. Ideally, you should meet with the other speakers and discuss in detail who will be covering what. If the co-presenters are from within your own firm or organisation, this should be easy to arrange; more problems can arise if you are speaking at a public conference. In the latter case, you should ask the organiser to provide as much of this information for you as possible and many will, as a matter of course, set up meetings of speakers. The trauma a speaker can experience on hearing most of his or her carefully prepared points being delivered by another speaker on the programme can easily be imagined.

6.2.2   The venue

In good time before the presentation you should be familiar with the venue for the presentation and you should make sure your audience knows how to get there. Issue them with maps if needs be. You will need to find out the physical characteristics of the room, namely, the sight-lines, the acoustics and the lighting.

If you are using visual aids in your presentation, you must make sure they will be visible to the whole of the audience. This will not be a problem in the case of most rooms used for presentations; the most frequent cause of blocked sight-lines is the presenter standing in front of the visual aid. Nevertheless, you may find you are presenting in an oddly shaped room or a room with pillar supports. If so, you must bear this in mind when positioning the seating and the visual aids.

It is self-evident that you must be audible when you make your presentation but will the room itself help or hinder your audibility? The rooms you are likely to use for client meetings are not likely to cause a problem in this regard. Similarly, purpose-built conference halls are designed to ensure excellent acoustics. The problems may arise if you are using a large room that was not designed as a venue for presentations. In good time before the presentation you should test the room's acoustics by positioning yourself wherever in the room you will be making the presentation. You should then say something, anything, with your voice pitched at 'presentation volume' and have a colleague check you are audible from all parts of the room where the audience will be sitting. You may find that rooms have unexpected pockets of poor acoustics (for example, if they are oddly shaped or near to air-conditioning vents). Even if you think the acoustics are satisfactory when you test them using your normal presentation volume, you should remember to *increase* that volume if the audience is large. The extra bodies in the room will absorb sound and you need to overcome this. When you are checking the acoustics, it is worth noting if the room is likely to be subject to external noise, for example, from a nearby street or neighbouring rooms. If you decide there will be a problem with the acoustics, you should either remember to project your voice more loudly or use an amplification system.

The lighting of the room is not likely to be a significant issue if you are dealing with a client meeting, save that out of politeness, for example, you should ensure the client is not blinded by the sun shining into his or her eyes. The lighting is more important when you are giving a more formal presentation. The purpose of checking the lighting is, obviously, to ensure that the audience can see what is going on. This covers both ensuring that the overhead lighting is adequate for the presentation and ensuring that the lighting in the room does not negate the impact of your visual aids. If you are using visual aids, the lighting in the room can adversely affect the impact of overhead projector slides, 35 mm slides and videos. You must, therefore, check the venue by testing your visual aids before the presentation. If these visual aids are not visible or easily visible when the room's lighting is on its normal setting, can you draw any blinds? Can you turn off some or all of the overhead lighting? If the overhead lighting dominates your visual aids, the simple solution would be to turn the overhead lighting off. This may, however, have the effect of darkening the room to the extent that although the visual aids are very visible, the audience cannot see to take notes. Accordingly, if it is possible, it is best to darken the room in zones so that the lights affecting the visual aids can be turned off or dimmed while retaining lighting in other parts of the room. If you are going to be turning the lights off, do you know where the switches are? Will they be easily accessible during the presentation?

6.2.3   The layout of the room

Chapter 3 described the various alternative training methods you could adopt for your presentation, ranging from the talking-head approach through to role-plays. Once you have decided on the most appropriate style for the presentation, you must ensure the room is laid out appropriately.

Therefore, where you are making a presentation to a large audience, you will probably have no choice but to seat them in rows. Do you then want them to have tables (classroom style) or only chairs (theatre style)?

If the audience is small, you should consider laying the tables and chairs out in a U-shape. This has the advantage of you being able to move among the audience and so reduce the barriers between you and them.

If the approach you have decided to adopt involves discussion groups, the room should be laid out so as to facilitate this approach. This will involve arranging tables which will suit the size of each group you wish to create. These tables should be physically separated from each other by a sufficient distance so that one discussion group does not disturb another. If this is a problem, you should organise, if possible, for one or more of the discussion groups to go into another room. (These rooms are sometimes called 'syndicate' or 'break-out' rooms.)

The most obvious illustration of a group discussion is a client meeting where the layout will probably be predetermined. It is, however, worthwhile giving thought to the way you seat the client (or clients) since you should ensure the layout minimises any barriers between you. In figures 6.1, 6.2 and 6.3, the crosses indicate possible seating positions.

Figure 6.1

The layout in figure 6.1 has the table as a barrier between the two participants to the meeting. It is more appropriate to a negotiation between two opposing parties than a meeting between a lawyer and his or her client.

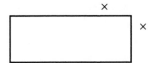

Figure 6.2

The layout in figure 6.2 minimises the barrier between the lawyer and the client. It has the advantage of enabling them to look at each other while having something on which to rest papers. This is probably the best layout to adopt when you are obtaining information from the client or giving advice on possible solutions to the client's problems.

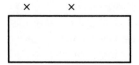

Figure 6.3

The layout in figure 6.3 is the most collaborative of the possible layouts in that there is no barrier at all between the lawyer and the client. However, it may be difficult to maintain eye contact. It is probably most appropriate when the purpose of the meeting is for the lawyer to go through a document with the client.

Where the meeting is with more than one other person, these suggested layouts may be less easy to use. You should, nevertheless, bear them in mind when seating the various people attending such larger meetings.

You should not only give thought to how you will seat the audience but also how you will position yourself. This is usually a decision easily taken since you will be standing at the front of the room near the visual aids. You should, however, give thought to whether it is appropriate for you to have a table or lectern in front of you. This probably will be appropriate for more formal presentations, but if you are trying to create the feeling of informality and endeavouring to engender audience participation, you should remove as many of the barriers between you and the audience as possible.

6.2.4   Equipment

If you have followed the advice in this book, you will be using some form of visual aid, most probably a flip chart, an overhead projector and/or a 35 mm projector. If that is the equipment you have decided upon, you should check that it will be available in the room on the day. Merely checking that there will be, for example, a flip chart and/or an overhead projector beforehand is not necessarily enough. Suppose you have prepared a set of flip-chart sheets which you will work your way through in the course of the presentation. It can be something of a surprise to discover the flip chart which the organiser has assured you will be available is screwed to the wall with the result that it is not possible to flip each sheet over the back. This will not be a problem if you do not intend referring to a particular flip-chart sheet once you have finished with it. However, it is a real problem if you intended going backwards and forwards between flip-chart sheets as part of your presentation. The degree of magnification achieved by overhead projectors is determined by how far the projector is away from the screen. You need to check whether the magnification is sufficient for your purposes.

If you know the equipment will be available and is suitable, on the day you should make sure it is in working order and that you know how to work it.

Although this may seem to be taking matters too far, it may be sensible to take with you a set of flip-chart and overhead projector pens and even a spare bulb for the OHP.

6.3 DURING THE PRESENTATION

If you have had an opportunity to prepare properly for the presentation (including time to rehearse) and also follow the guidelines given in 6.2, the problems you face will be minimal or even non-existent. Nevertheless, even with careful preparation and fore-thought, problems can still arise.

6.3.1 Disturbances

It is almost inevitable that disturbances will occur during presentations you give. These can be relatively minor, such as a noise from outside. While they may momentarily break the audience's concentration, they should not seriously inconvenience you (unless the noise is constant, for example, from a nearby building site). It is, however, worthwhile repeating the point you were making when you were interrupted.

A more common cause of disturbance is members of the audience arriving late or leaving early. While this is unlikely to happen at client meetings or beauty parade presentations, it is very likely to happen at more formal presentations such as public lectures. This kind of disturbance can be extremely disruptive. To minimise the problems which can be caused, you should know where the entrance to the room is. If the entrance is behind you, you are more likely to be surprised than if the entrance is at the back of the room behind the audience. There is a natural temptation for a late arrival or early leaver to apologise to the speaker. You should resist the temptation to engage in a conversation with the individual; merely acknowledge the apology and continue your presentation uninterrupted.

6.3.2   Loss of train of thought

Whether you are endeavouring to speak off the cuff or carefully following a prepared script, it is easy to lose your train of thought. While this can induce a rising sense of panic, the best way of dealing with it is to take time to find the next point you wish to make from your notes or script and then continue rather than drawing attention to the problem by some comment. To you, it may seem an eternity until you remember the next point you wish to make; the audience will probably have barely noticed the hiatus in your presentation.

6.3.3   Timing difficulties

If you have prepared and rehearsed properly, you should have a good idea of how long it will take you to deliver your presentation. However, you will find that when you are presenting to a real audience your presentation often takes longer than when you rehearsed it. This can be for a variety of reasons. As you were presenting, you may have seen that the audience did not understand a particular point and so rephrased it for clarity. You may have taken questions during the presentation which will have eaten into the time available. If you are trying to speak off the cuff, you will not necessarily have used exactly the same form of wording you used when you rehearsed and so may have unconsciously extended the length of the presentation.

If you do find yourself in this position, you should do your best to finish within the allotted time, whether or not you are the sole presenter.

If you are up against a tight time schedule, you will be keeping an eye on the time and you should know at any given moment in your presentation the point in your notes or script you should have reached. Therefore, when you are going through your full dress rehearsal, you should mark on your notes or script at regular intervals how long it took you to reach that part of the presentation. If 15 minutes into a 30-minute presentation you are dealing with points which you covered, when rehearsing, only 10 minutes into the presentation, you can be fairly certain you are going to overrun. What should you do about this? You could simply speed up your presentation but this is likely to reduce its effectiveness. The alternative approach is to omit information you had intended to cover. There are dangers with this approach. If you have not planned for this eventuality, you will have to choose which particular section of your presentation to omit, perhaps without adequate thought. You may then discover that the section you dropped needed to be covered if the audience are to understand a crucial point you make later in your presentation. When you reach that crucial point, you are faced with the problem that you cannot make that point without giving them the information you omitted. This can only lead to confusion on both sides, and a loss of credibility for you. The solution is to identify *in advance* points in your notes or script which you can safely omit without having any adverse effect on the overall impact of your presentation. If you have done this, you can drop these points from the presentation and hopefully catch up on the timetable.

Having too much information to cover in the time available is a problem. So is having too little if it means that you underrun your allocated time *substantially*. If you have prepared and rehearsed properly you should be able to deliver your presentation more or less in the time allocated to you. No significant problems will arise if you finish a 45-minute presentation a few minutes early, nor are problems likely to arise if you manage to beat a self-imposed deadline for a presentation at a meeting at which you are the only speaker. In both those circumstances, any time saved can probably be effectively filled by answering questions, even ones which you have posed yourself (see 6.4).

Problems can arise where, for example, you underrun your time when your presentation is part of a series of presentations. Will the next speaker be ready to start his or her presentation early? If you have underrun, have you dealt with all the points the audience anticipated to hear from you or have you left gaps in the coverage?

If you find yourself in this position of having exhausted your material but not your time slot, there is comparatively little you can do. You could ask for questions but this may highlight the problem if no question session is programmed at this point in the day. You may be able to use the imminent availability of coffee, lunch or tea as a way of filling the time but again it may look odd to the audience if a break programmed for 15 minutes is suddenly extended to, say, 30 minutes. If you unexpectedly find yourself in the position of having to fill time, the best approach is to develop the themes you did manage to cover in your presentation. There are obvious dangers in this approach. If you have not anticipated this as a possible problem, your comments will probably be unstructured and confused. To be on the safe side, you should, therefore, have prepared for this eventuality. In the same way that you should identify points which can be omitted when you are *over*running, you should hold in reserve some points to deliver if you are *under*running. If you have prepared properly, you can add these points into your presentation as you go through it rather than having to deliver them at the end.

6.3.4 Physical difficulties

It is inevitable that you may find yourself in physical difficulties during the presentation in the sense of getting a frog in your throat, suffering from a coughing fit or the like. It is far better to stop the presentation and resolve the problem than try to carry on regardless.

Although this hardly needs to be said, you should avoid creating problems for yourself. Therefore, you should *never* arrive late for a presentation as this will get you off to a bad start. If you have had to hurry to the presentation, you are hardly likely to present a good image if you are breathing heavily and sweating hard. On a less extreme note, it is worthwhile being careful what you eat and drink before the presentation. For example, it is worthwhile avoiding any drink with milk in it and eating chocolate as this can create mucus which will prohibit clear enunciation. The other problems to avoid with regard to food and drink are self-evident.

6.3.5   Replacing another speaker

One of the worst potential problems you can face during a presentation is to have to deliver the presentation on behalf of someone else. There are many circumstances when this can arise, for example, when you have to take the place of one of your colleagues who is unexpectedly unable to attend a client meeting. If a formal presentation has been arranged some time in advance, it may be difficult or impossible to change it if one of the speakers is unwell or otherwise unable to deliver his or her presentation.

How do you deal with such a situation? If the meeting you have to attend is the first meeting on a new matter with the client, this should not cause any problems if your technical expertise is the same as your missing colleague's. There is more likely to be a problem when you are standing in for a colleague at a formal presentation. If your colleague has prepared for the presentation, he or she should have a set of notes or a verbatim script which you can use.

If you merely have your colleague's notes, they may give you an idea of how to approach the presentation. If there is time, you should use the notes merely as a starting-point for going through the *full* preparation process explained in this book. Come what may, you should resist the temptation of trying to deliver the presentation in the same way as your colleague would have done. The audience will not thank you for delivering a pale imitation of the presentation your colleague would have made. The audience would prefer it if you made the presentation in your own style. Naturally, the audience may be disappointed if a late substitution is made for a particular speaker but you should think very carefully before apologising for being the replacement. If you do, you may leave the audience with the incorrect impression that you are less able than the colleague you are replacing.

Inheriting the full script your colleague has prepared for the presentation would seem to make your job easier. In reality, the dangers you face are greater than if you merely have his or her notes. With a verbatim script, the natural temptation would be simply to read it out. If you succumb to that temptation, you will be a very pale imitation of the first-choice presenter. Even with a verbatim script, preparation is still needed. You should make sure you both understand and agree with the points in the script. You should feel free to amend the script if you disagree with the order or phrasing. Again, resist apologising to the audience for replacing your colleague. Let them assess you on the merits of the presentation which you will, hopefully, have had time to make your own.

6.3.6   Chairing a presentation

What if you are chairing the presentation, whether at a beauty parade, a client meeting or a conference?

As the chair, it is your task at the beginning of the presentation to introduce the whole presentation and to introduce the speakers. When you do this, you should make sure you have discussed with them what you are going to say about them. You may have their full CVs but they may wish you to be selective in the information you give to the audience. In any event, you should help establish each speaker's credibility by saying a few words to explain why each speaker will be delivering his or her particular presentation.

Once the presentations begin, the likelihood is that you will sit at the front of the audience with or near to the speaker. If this is the case, you should avoid doing anything which may distract the audience from the speaker's presentation. You will be of most help to the presenter if you give the impression of listening with interest to whatever he or she is saying. As proof that your look of interest was not a mere sham, when the presenter has finished you could refer to particular points of interest or importance in the presentation before thanking the speaker for the presentation. Care should be taken when referring to points in the presenter's speech. You should not make comments which will detract from the impact of the presentation or which could confuse the audience about which are the key messages.

If any problems arise during the presentation, such as a speaker under or overrunning, you should take charge. You should be as supportive of your speaker as possible. Therefore avoid a brusque interruption to let the speaker know he or she is overrunning. It would be better if you unobtrusively drew the speaker's attention to the fact that time is moving on. If a speaker underruns, you may be able to redeem the situation by asking questions or entering into a discussion with the speaker to help fill the time.

Your final task when chairing the presentation will be to orchestrate the question session (whether there are such sessions at the end of each individual presentation or at the end of the full programme).

General guidance on handling questions is given in 6.4. When you are chairing a session, it will be your function to choose which questions to take and to direct which of the speakers will answer them. You should control the session in the sense of ensuring too much time is not devoted to one particular question or questioner.

It may be helpful to your speakers if you ensure the question session goes well by, for example, having prepared some questions of your own to ask if none come from the audience. Even if the audience ask the questions, there may be few of them or they may be on such specific points as not to be of general interest. In this case, you might consider encouraging the panel of speakers to discuss issues of interest to the whole audience. This will be informative and may provoke additional questions from the audience. Finally, you should help out any particular speaker who is suffering from an unpleasant question (such as one which he or she cannot answer or one raised by an aggressive questioner) by, for example, redirecting the question to other members of the panel of speakers.

6.4 AFTER THE PRESENTATION: QUESTIONS

Once the presentation is over, the only problem you are likely to face is that of handling the questions raised by your audience.

You may feel more confident about handling questions raised by clients at meetings than you do about dealing with questions raised by the audience at more formal presentations. There are, nevertheless, some general points to bear in mind when dealing with *any* questions.

When you are asked a question, you lose control of the direction your presentation will take. You must handle this situation with care. If you have decided to take questions during the presentation (which is probably not advisable during formal presentations to large audiences), you should never feel obliged to answer a question if you think the point is best dealt with at a later stage in the presentation. You can deal with the questioner easily by saying that you will come back to his or her point later.

The question of controlling when you answer the question does not apply if you have completed your presentation and have asked the audience for questions. In that circumstance, you should deal with the questions as they are asked. However, there is the problem of there being no questions raised. This may be because the audience can genuinely think of none but equally may be because, for whatever reason, they are reluctant to ask their questions. To help, it may be worthwhile getting the question session going by raising a question yourself. You can do this along the lines of 'Once I was asked . . .' or 'A point which is often raised is . . .'. This device may seem a little artificial and therefore as an alternative you could plant a question with a friend in the audience or with one of your co-presenters.

When the question is asked you must take care to listen carefully to it. Having done so, you should *always* repeat the question back to the questioner. This has a number of benefits. First, you can be certain that the entire audience heard the question. Secondly, if you repeat the question back to the questioner, you can check that you understood it. Thirdly, by repeating the question back and getting the questioner's response, you will give yourself extra time to think and you may get inspiration so far as finding the answer is concerned.

The questions you will be asked will fall into two categories: those you can answer and those you cannot. On the face of it, a question in the former category does not seem to be a problem. However, you need to consider carefully how full your answer should be. An interesting (to you) question on a very detailed part of your presentation may be one you could dwell on for several minutes. Your answer may be of great use to the questioner but will it help the rest of the audience understand your presentation? You may find that many of them may have heard the question but not fully appreciated its impact (even though you should always endeavour to make sure that everyone in the audience understands each question asked). In that case, those members of the audience will certainly not understand your answer.

If the question shows that the questioner was not listening to your presentation or had fundamentally misunderstood it, you should deal with it courteously and not dismiss the questioner.

Unfortunately, not all questioners will be as courteous as you should be. How should you, therefore, handle the aggressive questioner (who may phrase his or her question along the lines of 'You have not considered . . ., have you?')? You should maintain your courteous approach in the face of such opposition. If you deal with the question sensibly and in a reasonable manner, you will probably win the audience on to your side as they will perceive the questioner as unreasonable. Many presentations are on topics on which widely differing views can validly be held. You should, therefore, anticipate that someone may disagree with your views. If you find yourself in this position, you should try to identify any common ground. There is, however, no point entering into a protracted argument as it may be unproductive and will certainly be time-wasting. If you find this type of questioner (or any other type) is persistent or hogging the question session, you should politely cut them off and take questions from other members of the audience.

The second category of questions you may face (those you cannot answer) can be more traumatic. It may be possible to minimise the risk of this happening by asking for written questions to be handed in before the question session. However, this approach can really only be used at formal day-long conferences. You should first consider why you cannot answer the question. If it is ignorance on your behalf, you may be guilty of an error in preparation about which little can be done at this stage. However, it may in fact be reasonable for you to be unable to answer the question if it is only peripherally relevant to your subject-matter.

Whether or not it is reasonable for you to be able to answer the question, how do you deal with it? A bold 'I do not know' is neither helpful nor impressive. If you should know the answer but, for example, your mind has gone blank, a useful device is to throw the question back to the questioner (or to the audience generally) and ask for their views. Anyone who has the courage to ask a question at a presentation will probably be willing to express views. The views expressed may give you some guidance as to the answer or the additional time may have cleared your mental block. If the question is clearly peripheral, there can be no harm in explaining that you have not made that particular connection in the past.

If you have no idea of the answer to the question and none of the devices explained above give you any help, it is best to come clean. If doing so is likely to damage your credibility severely, you could suggest to the questioner that this is a point which you will be happy to discuss with him or her on a one-to-one basis later.

Most of the issues outlined in this section of the chapter dealing with questions are more relevant to formal presentations than to client meetings. If a client raises a question which you cannot answer, whether at a meeting or over the telephone, the best approach is always to promise the client that you will check the point and come back with a definite answer (whether or not you have attempted to answer it at the meeting or on the telephone).

6.5   SUMMARY

The cause of most problems is lack of preparation. If preparation is done properly, the problems you are likely to face will be few and far between. Nevertheless, you should:

(a)   Check all aspects of the venue and the presentation pro-gramme.

(b)   Know how to deal with problems which may arise during the presentation.

(c)   Be able to handle in an efficient, effective and impressive way any questions you may be asked after the presentation.

Conclusion

Following the advice given in this book, the book has an introduction, a main body and, now, a conclusion.

Presentations can either be fun or frightful. Which of these your presentation will be will depend on how you have approached it. If the presentation is to be an enjoyable and useful experience for everyone involved, you as the presenter should:

(a) Gather all the relevant information about the subject-matter of the presentation and its audience.

(b) Structure the presentation so as to deliver your message or information in a way the audience will find enjoyable, informative and memorable.

(c) Rehearse the presentation before delivering it and make any improvements necessary.

(d) Deliver the presentation (including any question session) in a way that projects your personality, leaving the audience impressed with your grasp of the topic as well as both entertained and better informed.

With these general guidelines in mind, it is hoped you will find the presentations you give, whether over the telephone or face to face, whether to clients or colleagues and whether informal (at meetings) or formal (at lectures) to be trauma-free experiences.

Good luck!

Bibliography

Max Atkinson, *Our Masters' Voices* (Routledge, 1984).

Antony Jay, *Effective Presentation – The Communication of Ideas by Words and Visual Aids* (British Institute of Management, 1971).

Jacqueline Dunckel and Elizabeth Parnham, *The Business Guide to Effective Speaking* (Kogan Page, 1984).

Dorothy M. Stewart (ed.), *Handbook of Management Skills* (Gower Publishing, 1987).

In addition, there is a very useful video-based training package called *Complete Communication* produced by Melrose.